Film Actresses

Volume 21

Myrna Loy

Documentary study

Part 1

ISBN-13 : 978-1502975881

ISBN-10 : 1502975882

Dtp
and
graphic design

Iacob Adrian

Author statement

The actors and actresses are the the bricks .

The cast and crew are the plaster .

They stand on the foundation created by
producers and writers and directors .

All these people creates the great palace
of the art of film .

Iacob Adrian - 2013

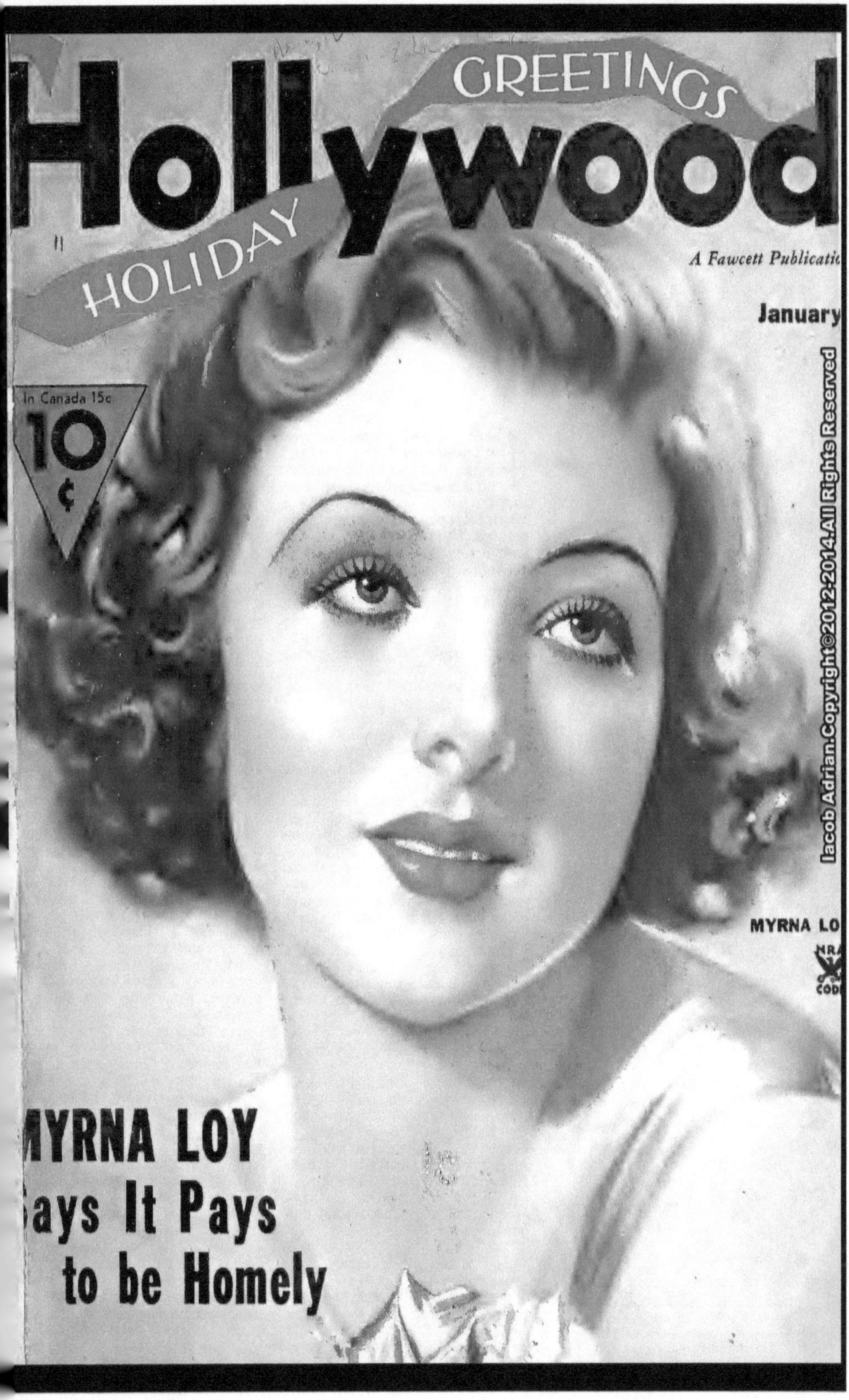

Hollywood

GREETINGS

HOLIDAY

A Fawcett Publication

January

In Canada 15c

10 ¢

MYRNA LO

NRA
CODE

MYRNA LOY
Says It Pays
to be Homely

Myrna Loy Says IT PAYS

by *Grace Mack*

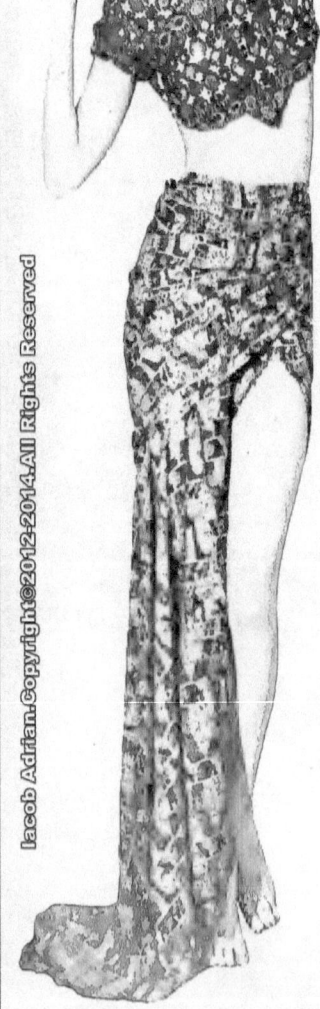

Rôles like the above imprisoned Myrna for years behind an oriental mask. She hated these exotic parts and bided her chance to escape.

"I'M GLAD THAT *I was born homely. It's the luckiest break I ever had.*"

Better read that again, you girls who think that homeliness is a handicap, for the author of that startling statement is none other than the very gorgeous Myrna Loy.

Naturally, you will wonder why anybody should be grateful for homeliness.

Here is Myrna's answer:

"Whether it's a career—or a man—I honestly believe that the girl who is born homely has a better chance to get what she wants than the girl who is born beautiful. For this reason: The girl who is born homely learns very early in life that if she wants her share of the world's plums she can't sit idly by and wait for them to fall into her lap. She has to get out and shake the tree. Whereas the girl who has been brought up to believe herself beautiful is too likely to regard her beauty as an all-powerful weapon with the result that she neglects to cultivate other charms. She never has to exert herself to attract people. Consequently, she fails to see the necessity of being interesting. And while it is true that a beautiful girl may attract a man, if she is dumb she seldom holds him. A homely girl, if she wants to get anywhere, knows that she doesn't dare to be dull and uninteresting. She has to use her head. And she has to learn to make the most of what she has.

● "It was not until I was about twelve years old," says Myrna, "that I bumped into the realization that Nature had done me wrong. I knew of course that my hair was straight and red, that I had a snub nose and a face splattered with freckles. It never occurred to me, however, that these things made any difference—*until I fell in love.*

"The object of my adoration was a boy named John Brown. He scarcely knew that I existed. To him I was just a red-headed, spindle-legged roughneck who threw stones and bloodied noses when anybody got fresh and called me 'Red' or 'Freckle-

Face.' He had eyes only for my playmate—a little girl named Jane.

"Jane had china-blue eyes and golden curls and a beautiful milk white skin. John would invite her to ride home on the handlebars of his bicycle, leaving me to tag along behind on foot. Each day I would think: 'Well, maybe he'll ask me tomorrow.' But he never did. Dimly I began to realize that it was because Jane was pretty and I was homely.

"Like every other girl, I wanted to be popular. I wanted to attract boys. It was obvious that I could never do it with my looks. I'd have to find some *substitute* for beauty. Then and there I decided that I would be a dancer or an actress. Looking back on it now, I know that my ambition was the result of the heartache that accompanied the discovery that I was an Ugly Duckling.

"In the years that followed I read every beauty article I could get my hands on. I began to massage my scalp and brush my hair and I learned to comb my hair in a way that was more becoming. I began to take care of my skin. I took a serious interest in my clothes. I worked like a dog at my dancing, for I knew that in order to compete with the girls who were pretty, I would have to be able to dance better than they did or I wouldn't stand a chance.

"And then one day I looked into the mirror and was suddenly aware that something had happened to me. My legs were not quite so spindly. My face was rounder and my hair had become fluffy. It even had the trace of a natural wave. I was quite astonished.

"'Why you don't look half-bad,' I told my reflection. 'Maybe there's hope for you yet.'

"Other people began to notice the change. 'What have you been doing to yourself, Myrna?' they asked. 'You're getting better looking.'

"A girl who is born beautiful becomes accustomed to being a receiving station for compliments. She accepts them as a matter of course. Only the girl who has taken the

TO BE HOMELY

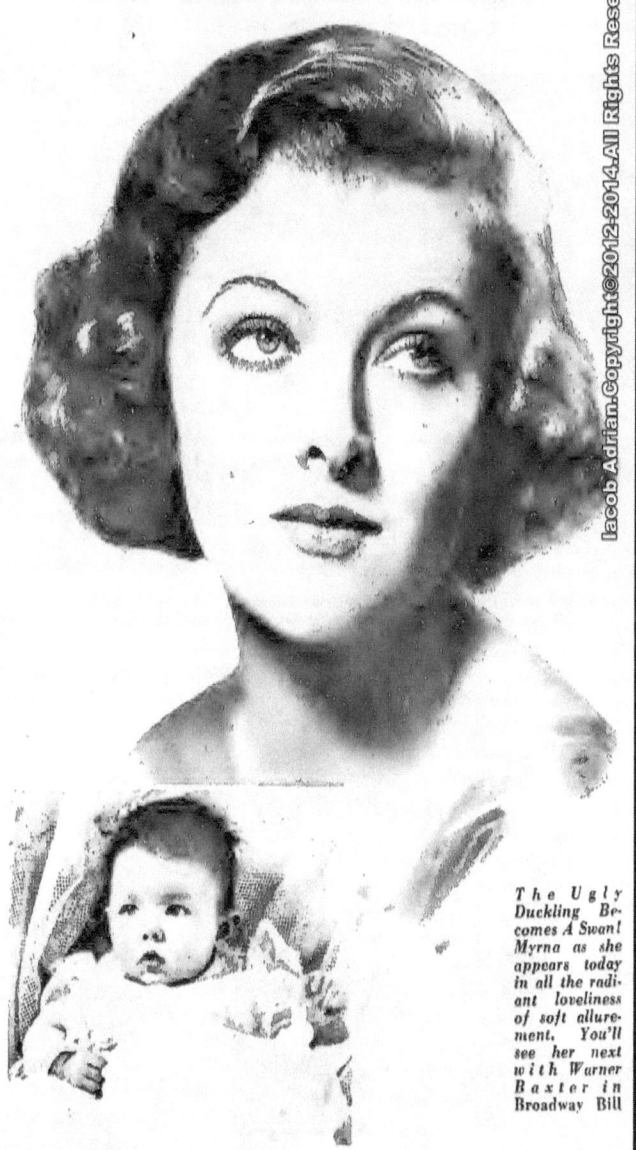

assortment of features which Nature handed her, and through patience and perseverance has managed to improve upon them, knows what a real shot in the arm a compliment can be. I simply glowed.

"It was not, however, until I was about sixteen that I felt absolutely paid in full for all the time and effort I had spent trying to improve myself. If my career had ended then and there I would have had no regrets . . . *Valentino had told me that I looked lovely!*

"Here is the story:

"I had my first job as a dancer, in a prologue at the Egyptian theatre in Hollywood. Henry Waxman, a photographer, came to the theatre to make some pictures of the girls. For some reason he thought I was an interesting photographic subject and he made numerous studies of me. Little did I dream that this seemingly inconsequential incident would be the means of opening the door of opportunity for me.

"A short time later, however, Valentino and his wife chanced—or *was* it chance?—to visit the Waxman studio. They saw my picture. Something about it intrigued them. Mr. Waxman showed him the other studies he had made. They told him they would like to have me come to their studio for an interview.

● "The day that I went to see Valentino will probably always remain one of the really big moments in my life. Like most girls of my generation, I was a Valentino addict. I had never missed seeing one of his pictures. The thought of actually seeing him in person and talking with him simply sent gooseflesh racing up and down my spine.

"I met Natacha first. I thought she was the most beautiful thing I had ever seen. I felt like a plain little mouse in her presence and I was terribly frightened. Then Valentino came into the room. He was so charming and natural that he immediately made me feel at ease.

"He explained that they wanted to make a test of me. Natacha loaned me a beautiful gown for the test. But there seemed to be no place for me

The Ugly Duckling Becomes A Swan! Myrna as she appears today in all the radiant loveliness of soft allurement. You'll see her next with Warner Baxter in Broadway Bill

Myrna's homeliness doesn't seem to have started yet in this picture which shows her at the age of eight months. But then all babies are cute!

BROADWAY BILL

Myrna Loy, Warner Baxter and a wonderful horse in a gripping thriller of the race track

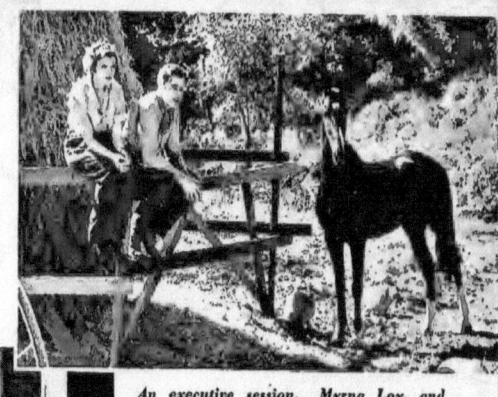

An executive session. Myrna Loy, and Warner Baxter discuss plans for the big sweepstakes with Broadway Bill cocking an attentive ear

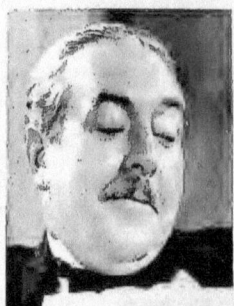

Genial Walter Connolly, the tycoon of Higginsville and father-in-law of Baxter

The long arm of the law adds to Baxter's misfortunes when he is arrested for fighting and non-payment of feed bills on the eve of the race

Chances of winning the sweepstakes seem very slight to Baxter but Myrna is trying her best to console him

Myrna Loy says it Pays to be Homely

to change. Finally Valentino said: 'Let her use my portable dressing room. I won't be needing it.'

"You girls who carried the torch for Valentino won't need to be told how thrilled I was to dress before his mirror. Natacha's gown and makeup did wonders for me. In fact, it seemed to me as I stared at my reflection that in some magical way I had been transformed into a person who bore no resemblance whatever to the homely little roughneck of a few years previous.

"Breathlessly, I went out to let them look me over. I shall never forget Valentino's comment. 'You look perfectly lovely,' he said.

"Only a girl who has cried herself to sleep at night because she was homely will appreciate what that compliment meant to me. For days I went around with my head in the clouds. Seeing the test, however, jerked me back to earth with a bang. I looked simply awful on the screen. My cheeks seemed sunken and my eyes were like dark blots. My teeth were conspicuously bad. I moved so fast and jerky across the screen that I resembled a Keystone comedy. I realized that bad lighting had been partially responsible but that knowledge was poor consolation. I ran out of the projection room, my eyes filled with tears. There was just one thought in my mind: I had failed, and failed miserably.

"I know now that that experience was the greatest lesson I ever had for out of that crushing humiliation grew a de-

termination not to give up until I had reached my goal."

"SOME TIME LATER Natacha sent for me. She never mentioned the test. She merely said that they were confident that I could be developed into an odd screen personality and that she wanted to use me in her picture *What Price Beauty*. She showed me the sort of makeup to use, taught me to slant my eyebrows, and to give my mouth a sensual curve. She dressed me in bizarre costumes. Her belief in me gave me new confidence in myself. The result was that gradually I evolved a new personality. The process was long and sometimes painful. It meant trying and failing and getting up and trying again. If I had been born beautiful I doubt if I would have had the courage to see it through.

"Please don't conclude that I am stupid enough to underestimate the value of beauty. It is indeed a precious thing. But, as Aldous Huxley once pointed out, the greatest source of beauty is an experiencing soul. The perfection of eyes and nose and mouth can be utterly *blah* if there's nothing else to go with it.

"When Nature has done all the work for a girl there is really nothing to spur her on. Whereas a face or a figure that needs a lot of work done on it is a direct challenge. I firmly believe that any girl who will use her head can create an *illusion* of beauty. It simply means discovering what her best points are and then playing them up for all they're worth. It can be a lot of fun, too. *I know—because I've tried it.*"

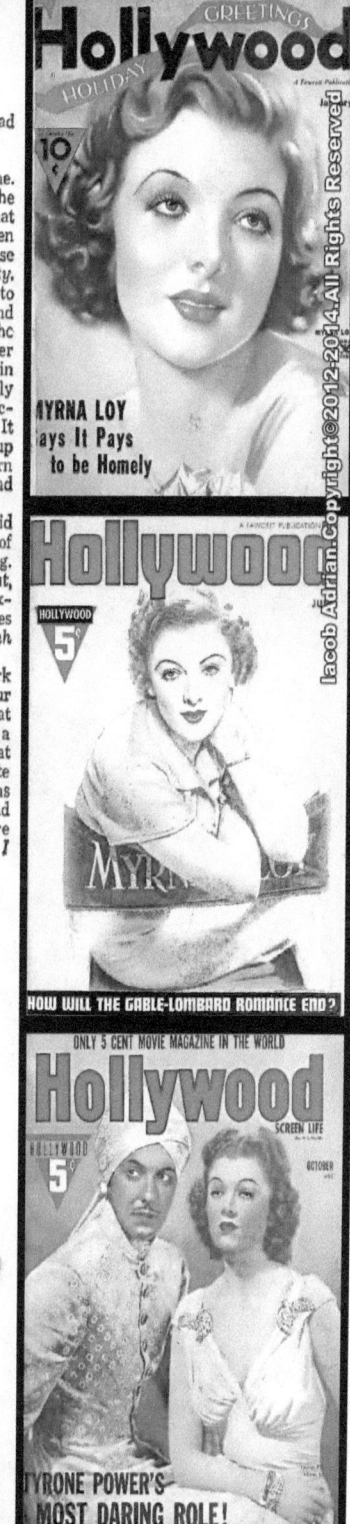

MYRNA LOY
ays It Pays
to be Homely

HOW WILL THE GABLE-LOMBARD ROMANCE END?

TYRONE POWER'S MOST DARING ROLE!

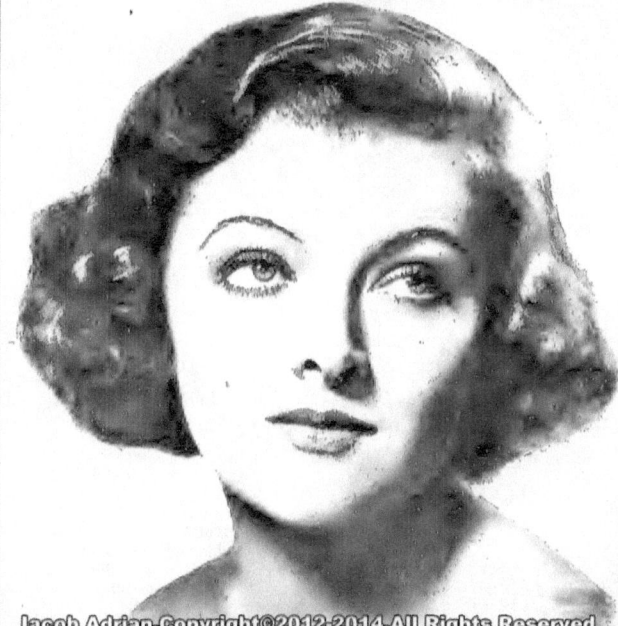

Why Myrna Loy is a Bachelor Girl

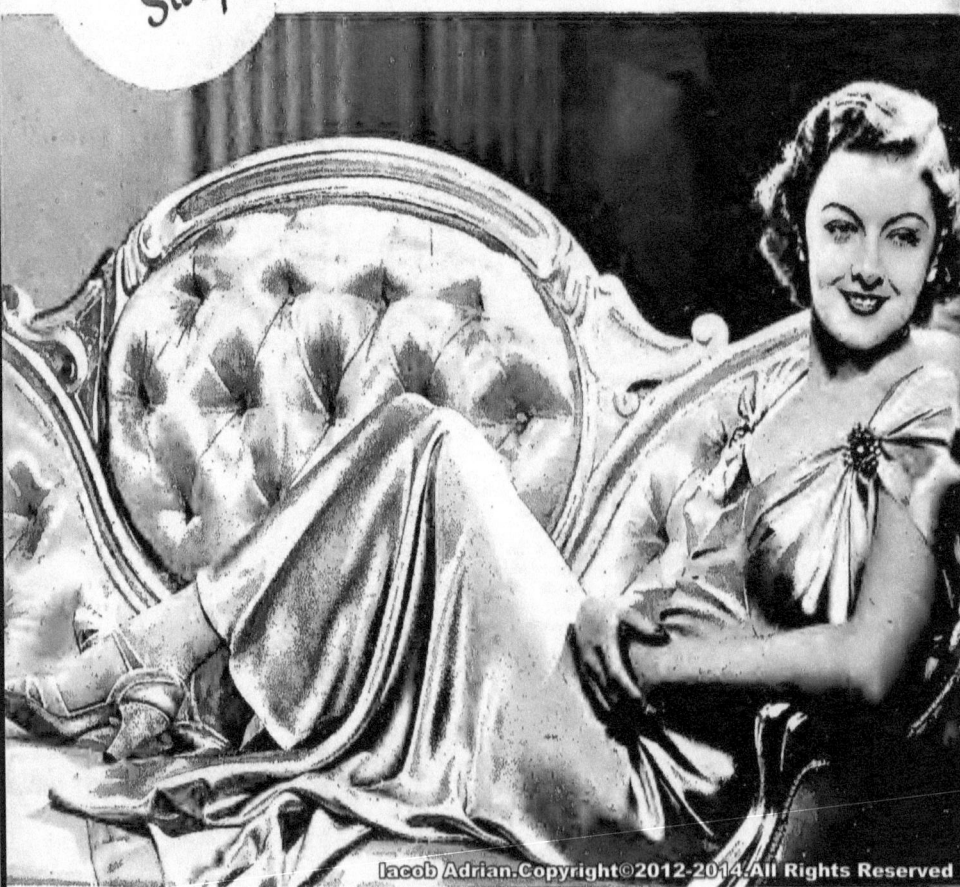

● MYRNA LOY has become one of Hollywood's favorite mysteries.

No one seems to know anything about her. No one has been able to catch her off-guard, without her smiling, imperturbable and freckled mask. In her own studio she is a far greater mystery than Garbo. Because Garbo is what she's supposed to be, a strange, shy Swedish sphinx. But Myrna looks and acts and talks like a normal young woman. When Myrna suddenly stepped from the cocoon of Oriental rôles into the butterfly shimmer of modern heroines and Adrian gowns, Hollywood sat up and took a new interest in her. A hundred times, when

Here it is—our first Command Story, published in answer to hundreds of letters from readers asking for a really good interview with Myrna Loy. There will be Command Stories each issue, so let us know your preference

by ELEANOR PACKER

I worked in the crazy confusion of the Metro-Goldwyn-Mayer publicity department, people asked, "What sort of person is Myrna Loy? Oh, I know she's from Montana and doesn't look exotic off the screen. But what kind of a girl is she?"

One woman magazine editor came to Hollywood for a brief vacation and asked for an interview with Myrna. "Dozens of Loy stories have been sent to me," she explained. "But not one of them really tells anything about the girl. I'd like to see her away from the studio, in her own home. Maybe she'll break down and talk."

So it was arranged. The editor

Why Myrna Loy is a Bachelor Girl

spent a long afternoon with Myrna in her little hillside house. She came back to the studio, baffled and bewildered.

"We had a great time," she sighed, "Myrna talked and talked. But, when I walked out the front door, I realized that she hadn't told me a thing I didn't know about her. All I really learned from that interview was the recipe for the heavenly rolled sandwiches which we had with tea. And her cook gave me that."

Two of Hollywood's most formidable interviewers tackled her at one time. If one failed to find material for a story, the other surely would, they explained. They descended upon Myrna's studio dressing room with a grim determination in their faces. They came back to my office two hours later with blank eyes and no story.

"She answered our questions," they chorused. "She talked about her work and the studio and music. She even gossiped a little, like any normal woman. But we couldn't find out one thing about her personal life or her own thoughts."

I always smile when people talk about the mystery of Garbo. Compared to Myrna Loy, Garbo's life is an open book. Myrna doesn't publicize her mystery. She doesn't admit it. She denies it.

"I'm not trying to be secretive or mysterious," she told me, "I'm simply scared to death of interviews. I tremble inside and can't think of anything to say. I want to give them interesting stories, but I don't know how to do it."

Myrna may believe that. And she may not. But I know that she's wrong. She can be a most fluent conversationalist—when she chooses. When the discussion is impersonal and general, Myrna talks easily and often brilliantly. But, when it swerves into personal channels, she becomes smilingly silent. Not rudely. Not abruptly. Merely firmly and solidly like a stone wall. You can batter your head against it, as long as you have strength, but it will not break.

Myrna is diabolically clever. Women would be wiser, and perhaps happier, if they would learn her lesson of well-timed silence. One afternoon I watched Myrna turn an experienced newspaper woman from a carefully planned attack against Myrna's private life into a discussion of ancient and modern surgery. She concluded the interview by looking at Myrna's collection of medical books. The woman left without learning the answer to the question which she had come to ask. Are you in love with a certain actor?

All Hollywood knows that Myrna is in love with some one. She has that look of a woman, loved and loving. Everyone seems to know who it is. But everyone mentions a different name. An actor. Another actor. A director. A producer. A business man. A writer. A half dozen others.

After several years of knowing and watching Myrna, I've finally decided that there is nothing really mysterious about her.

Myrna is a pioneer in the true New Freedom for women. She makes the "bachelor girls" of yesterday look like silly, noisy mimics of masculinity. There is nothing blatant or masculine about Myrna and her creed. She is utterly feminine. She is, I honestly believe, the successful and charming spinster of today and tomorrow.

Myrna does what so many other women would like to do, but haven't the courage to try. She disproves the old saying, "Love is to man's life, a thing apart. 'Tis woman's whole existence." Myrna manages to keep her love apart from her professional life. She never mentions love. When she is in the studio, she ignores the life in the hillside house as if it had no existence. Her work is all-important then. She loves it. Probably, away from the studio, her other life becomes all-important. I don't know. No one does, except the mysterious few who share it with her. Myrna kills all scandal because she gives it no meat upon which to feed.

● ONCE A well-meaning young press agent, searching for his quota of paragraphs for the daily newspaper columns, wrote that when Myrna was suddenly called for work one night, she asked her maid to phone two men to break her engagements with them. A newspaper printed the little item. Myrna was courteously but vigorously upset about it. In the first place, it was untrue. The young man had thought that he was enhancing Myrna's romantic popularity. In the second place, it was an intrusion upon that other life away from the studio. If Myrna had other reasons for her displeasure, she didn't mention them. But you and I know that, if there is one man of importance to her, and there must be, he would not like the public mention of another.

One day I went to Myrna's home for luncheon. She had just returned from a vacation. No one knew where she had been, but we supposed the desert. It was winter and Myrna loves the sun. She was living at that time in a house in Brentwood, which she had rented, furnished. The house was set far back from the quiet street and presented a blind, white stucco front to passers-by. But the living room windows opened onto a wide terrace and a walled garden, set high on a bluff, where Myrna could lie in the sun and see, without being seen.

I asked her about her vacation and she laughed, that low, rippling Loy laugh, which crinkles her slanting eyes.

"I've been right here at home all the time," she giggled, "Hiding out in my own house. Only three people, except the servants knew where I was."

She didn't tell me who the three people were. I wanted to ask. But I didn't.

We had fried chicken and hot biscuits on a card table before the blazing fire in the living room, while the noontime sunshine poured in through the open windows. There is nothing anemic about Myrna's appetite. She enjoys her food with a healthy gusto, born of her Montana childhood, when she was a skinny, little girl with carroty braids pulled back tightly from her freckled face. That is Myrna's own description of her younger tomboy self.

I had gone to that luncheon, determined to break through the barrier of Myrna's silence. I learned just three things. She was in love, quietly, glintingly in love. She hoped, of course, to marry some day. She had never been in New York.

A few weeks later I talked to Myrna in a Hollywood apartment. She had left the Brentwood house when its owners returned. She hated the apartment. She felt as if she were living in a gold fish bowl. Her neighbors could see and know everything which she did. She could see and hear them. She couldn't play her favorite records after midnight and Myrna loves music in the wee, small hours. The apartment house was a fashionable one, filled with people from the various studios. It brought her two lives too close together.

So Myrna found another house with complete seclusion for a modern spinster who wants to live her own life in her own way. It was set far back in a high-walled canyon. Myrna left the owner's name on the mail box at the edge of the street.

Until two years ago Myrna lived with her mother, her younger brother and an aunt. Then her mother went to Europe and Myrna moved into a home of her own. She settled down to a new order of living. When her mother returned, Myrna continued to live alone. That was a part of the freedom which Myrna had learned to demand and to achieve. She sees her family several times a week.

A few months ago Hollywood thought that, at last, it had glimpsed the Myrna behind the mask. She was in love with Ramón Novarro and the romance was not veiled in secrecy. They played together in The Barbarian and, when the picture was finished, they went here and there together. Ramón departed for a European concert tour and Myrna moved into his home during his absence. Everyone, who could reach Myrna, asked the same question, "Are you going to marry Ramón when he returns?" And everyone received the same answer, a puzzling, enigmatic smile. Myrna neither affirmed nor denied the rumors of serious romance.

● Ramón returned. Myrna did not meet him at the station. But Ramón went to her home—she had, of course, moved from his house—as soon as he had greeted his family. They dined together frequently. Myrna talked freely of her friendship and admiration for Ramón. "He is a constant source of amazement to me," she said, "You never know what Ramón you will find. Sometimes he is a silly, crazy, charming boy. Again he is a mature, thoughtful, almost melancholy man. He is one of my closest friends." The rumors of romance died because there was nothing to nourish them. They were replaced by whispers that the Novarro romance was merely a part of the Loy mask. Myrna is the only one who knows the truth.

Myrna's studio dressing room suite, two rooms and a shower, is at the end of the second story of the long frame building which houses the Metro-Goldwyn-Mayer players. At the opposite end of the narrow balcony are the quarters of Greta Garbo, the other and more publicized Sphinx. But the greater of the two, I believe, is Myrna. Because her sphinxness is cloaked in a smiling friendliness and a healthy American appearance of frank candor.

Myrna has given up her dancing and sculpture, the two careers which she planned before Rudolph Valentino and his wife discovered her and introduced her to motion pictures. Myrna reads constantly and knows more about medical science than the average layman. She liked working in Men in White, because hospitals and doctors' offices fascinate her.

I have known Myrna for several years. I've talked to her hours on end, lunched with her, teaed with her, worked with her. She isn't a mystery. She is a young woman who has the courage of her convictions. But, still, sometimes I wonder—

Her One Big Moment

"I had ambitions to become a great dancer, and there WAS a high spot in my life when mother told me I could quit my studies at the Venice, Cal., high school and go into a spot in a Sid Grauman p r o l o g u e,"

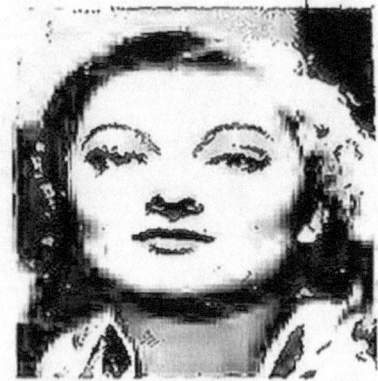

Myrna Loy

Myrna Loy says. "Soon after this, H e n r y Wax- man, a noted p h o t o g r a p h e r, taking note of the Oriental s l a n t of my eyes, made some s t r i k i n g por- traits of me. The late R u d o l p h Valentino noted the portraits and his wife, the beloved Natacha Rambova, after looking at the photo- graphs, urged Rudy to send for me. Then came the one big moment in my life——Mrs. Valentino took me in hand. I became her protégé.

"I had a series of heart breaking experiences," Miss Loy continued, "but eventually, under the guidance of Natacha, I began to click. So, here am I. But, to my dying day, I shall never forget that day when Natacha decided I was to be her protégé. THAT WAS MY BIG MOMENT."

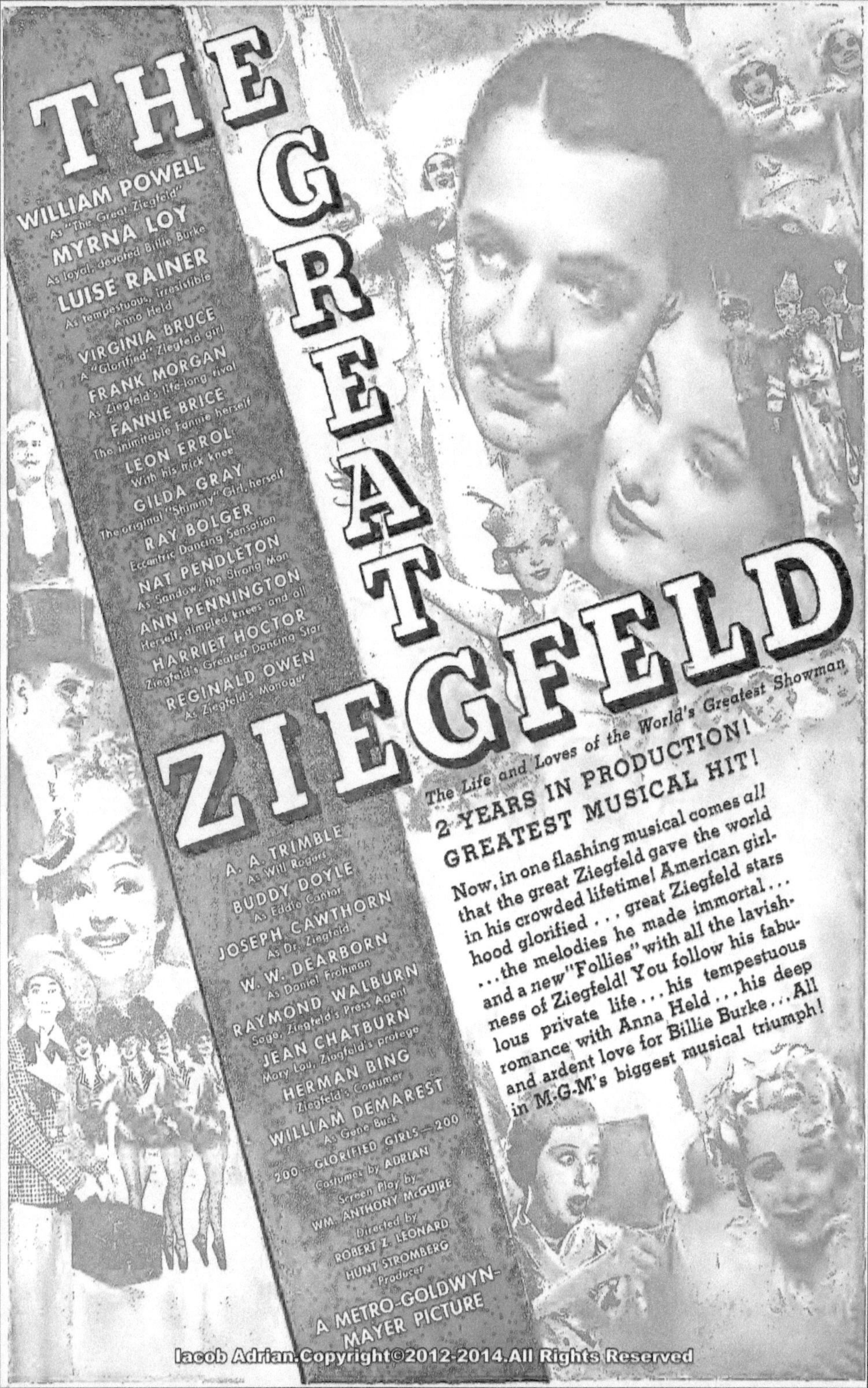

THE GREAT ZIEGFELD

WILLIAM POWELL
As "The Great Ziegfeld"

MYRNA LOY
As loyal, devoted Billie Burke

LUISE RAINER
As tempestuous, irresistible
Anna Held

VIRGINIA BRUCE
A "Glorified" Ziegfeld girl

FRANK MORGAN
As Ziegfeld's life-long rival

FANNIE BRICE
The inimitable Fannie herself

LEON ERROL
With his trick knee

GILDA GRAY
The original "Shimmy" Girl, herself

RAY BOLGER
Eccentric Dancing Sensation

NAT PENDLETON
As Sandow, the Strong Man

ANN PENNINGTON
Herself, dimpled knees and all

HARRIET HOCTOR
Ziegfeld's Greatest Dancing Star

REGINALD OWEN
As Ziegfeld's Manager

A. A. TRIMBLE
As Will Rogers

BUDDY DOYLE
As Eddie Cantor

JOSEPH CAWTHORN
As Dr. Ziegfeld

W. W. DEARBORN
As Daniel Frohman

RAYMOND WALBURN
Sage, Ziegfeld's Press Agent

JEAN CHATBURN
Mary Lou, Ziegfeld's protege

HERMAN BING
Ziegfeld's Costumer

WILLIAM DEMAREST
As Gene Buck

200—GLORIFIED GIRLS—200
Costumes by ADRIAN
Screen Play by
WM. ANTHONY McGUIRE
Directed by
ROBERT Z. LEONARD
HUNT STROMBERG
Producer

A METRO-GOLDWYN-
MAYER PICTURE

ZIEGFELD

The Life and Loves of the World's Greatest Showman

2 YEARS IN PRODUCTION!
GREATEST MUSICAL HIT!

Now, in one flashing musical comes all that the great Ziegfeld gave the world in his crowded lifetime! American girl-hood glorified . . . great Ziegfeld stars . . . the melodies he made immortal . . . and a new "Follies" with all the lavish-ness of Ziegfeld! You follow his fabu-lous private life . . . his tempestuous romance with Anna Held . . . his deep and ardent love for Billie Burke . . . All in M-G-M's biggest musical triumph!

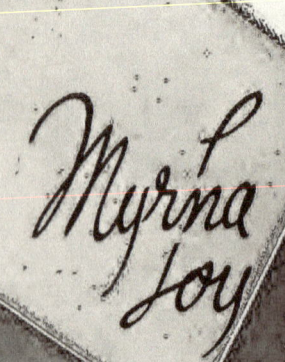

Myrna
Loy

Myrna Loy faces the New
Year with every reason to be
happy! Eminently success-
ful in M-G-M's *Libeled
Lady*, she is ready to shoot
at new box office records

Myrna Loy's Hand Carved Career!

Myrna Loy is a sculptress. She is also a painter. And she can play the piano. As a dancer she has few equals and still fewer superiors in all Hollywood. Which gives you a few ideas of her talents outside the field of acting, where any comment would be superfluous.

But Myrna's greatest piece of sculpturing has not been in the field of marble or plaster. It has been in the shaping of her own life and career to the point where she stands out as the envy of other women the world over. The Loy she has moulded in the flesh will remain a monument to the determination of a little girl, from the cattle plains of Montana, who early in life promised herself to make good in Hollywood and who fulfilled that promise to the very letter.

When you see her in *After the Thin Man* or in *Parnell*, her two latest films for Metro-Goldwyn-Mayer, you will not be viewing a child of destiny. You will be seeing a great actress created through her own efforts and spirit.

Let's look back over the years and see how all this has happened. It is interesting and not a little bit inspiring. Perhaps there is a formula which will help others mould their own careers and then fight through the maze of entanglements which seem to be a necessary part in any battle for success.

The record shows that a Myrna Williams came into the world at Helena, Montana, about 31 years ago. "Myrna Williams?" you ask. Yes, Myrna Williams. Her family was a typical American one, with the tang of Scotland's heather fields in its ancestry. Down the street, a few doors, lived another family, named Cooper. A son, Gary, was

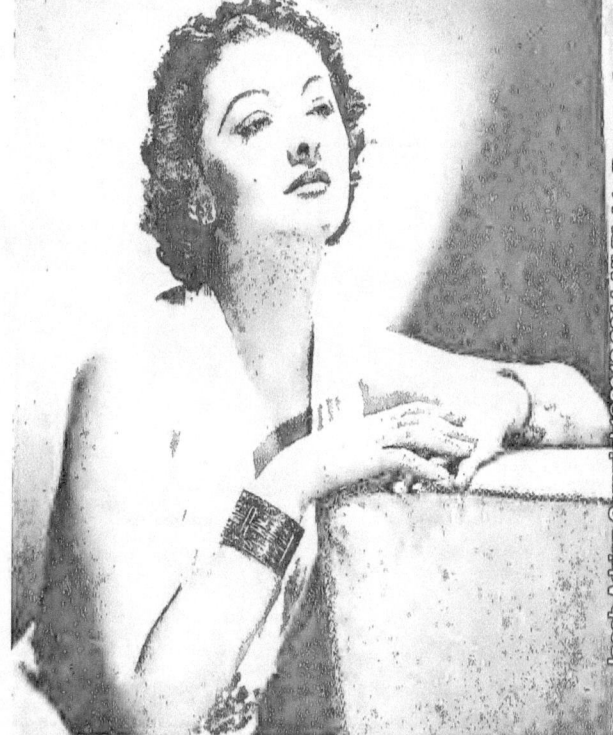

Charming Myrna Loy as she appears today after a decade of transition from half-caste to the ultimate of modern sophistication. Out of the chrysalis of past effort she emerges the envy of many women the world over

destined to achieve great fame in the cinema, but in those days he was just a little shaver playing tag with the other kids in the same block.

The fact that Gary Cooper lived in the same block has absolutely nothing to do with this story. It is merely an interesting commentary. It is doubtful if either Gary or Myrna can remember the other and in Hollywood they have had nothing more than a nodding friendship. All of which helps to prove that the world is a strange place, after all.

Modeling Came First

When the mother was widowed, she decided that she would go to California with her two children, Myrna and David. That was how Myrna Williams happened to become a model. All by accident, but undoubtedly it had much to do with her future.

Venice is a beach suburb of Los Angeles.

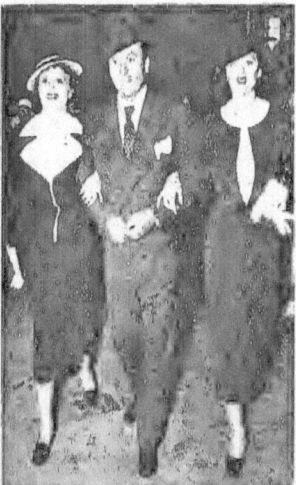

Here is Myrna Loy (right) with her husband, Arthur Hornblow, Jr., and Sharon Lynne as seen by cameraman at a Hollywood preview

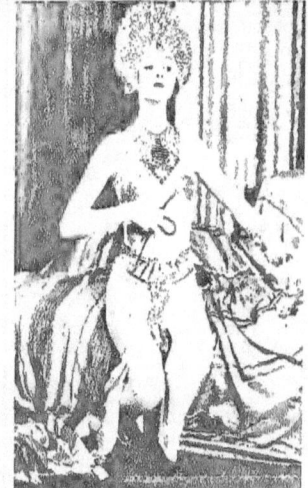

It is a far cry from the Myrna Loy of a half dozen years ago, when she was cast as an Oriental, to the glamorous film star of 1937

Myrna Loy's Career

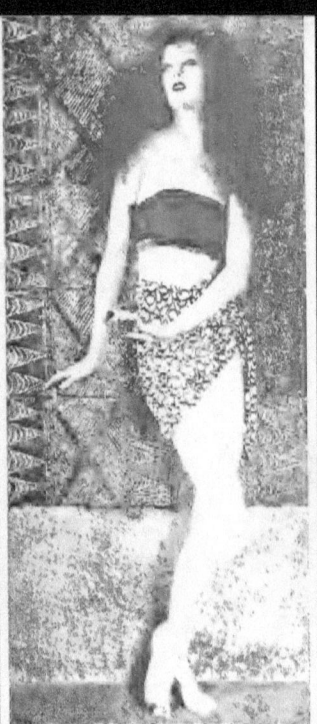

Myrna Loy's transition from a dancing girl in a Sid Grauman prologue to the feminine star of *After the Thin Man*, is a gap such as very few of her sex ever have bridged

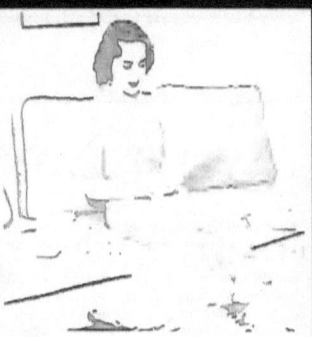

She likes to read fan letters! Olivia de Havilland never fails to see what her countless friends have to suggest through the mails!

Like all other small communities, it is very proud of its high school. Out in front of the school there is a statue which represents the Physical, the Mental and the Spiritual. The sculptor had an easy time finding an athlete to pose for the Physical. He found someone who could pose for the Mental, but finding a model for the Spiritual was a task. Myrna Williams, for the first time in her life, stepped out to help herself. She readily understood the honor and distinction of being chosen as the ideal Spiritual type. And when this demure little high school girl stood before him, the great man who was shaping the model for the statue knew that here was his ideal.

But Myrna imposed one condition. And a strange one it was, considering that she realized the honor of her selection. She demanded that if she posed, her true identity be kept secret!

That was the beginning of a strange policy which Myrna has always pursued. She doesn't mind being talked about, professionally, that is, but she is loathe to talk about herself. Quite a contrast from many other queens of the screen!

In high school, the little girl from Montana was principally interested in the arts. Somewhere, among the old class files, there can still be found those early drawings, those early mouldings. And the music rooms must still echo the tunes of the piano as she diligently practiced.

After Venice High School, there were the days in the Westlake School for Girls, a fashionable institution patronized largely by society families. Then Myrna Williams stepped out to face the world. Always adept at dancing, she now realized, for the first time, that mere wishing would not break down the walls between desire and accomplishment. If Myrna were to be a dancer, she wanted to be a great one. So she sought out Ruth St. Denis, one of the great dancers of the times and who was then conducting classes at her school in Los Angeles. The price came high, but the results were what Myrna wanted. After an hour's lesson, she would practice by the day to get full value out of it.

Dances in Prologue

In those days, Hollywood was just becoming the city of glamour that it now is. Sid Grauman, the great showman, had only recently left the downtown area of Los Angeles and opened Grauman's Egyptian Theatre in Hollywood. Now a second run house, it is only a reminder of the days when it was the best, and because of its exotic Egyptian setting, something of a sensation and a mecca for tourists. It was really the beginning of the glamorous Hollywood which is now known around the world.

Sid Grauman had at that time introduced the prologue, something entirely new in the motion picture theatre. It consisted of an elaborately staged show that tied into the theme of the picture being shown. Dancers were used in liberal numbers.

When she considered herself sufficiently trained, Myrna Williams went to the theatre, rapped on the stage door and landed a job in the chorus. It was a tough job as jobs go. Grauman is a severe task master. When a chorus dances for Grauman, it dances to perfection. That is

how he became the Ziegfeld of the west.

Myrna's particular type of beauty had attracted the attention of Henry Waxman, a famed photographer. He photographed her many times and then introduced her to Natacha Rambova, the wife of Rudolph Valentino. Myrna Williams knew this was the opportunity she had long awaited. And Natacha Rambova saw in the little dancing girl from Grauman's Egyptian theatre chorus that spark of greatness that would later flower into stardom and intrigue audiences the world over.

If Myrna Williams was anxious for a chance at the movies, Natacha Rambova was more anxious to help her get that chance. She saw to it that Myrna was given a big part in *What Price Beauty*.

That picture, as many will remember, was a great failure, so pronounced that it is still talked about within the studios. But it was Myrna Williams' long-awaited, long-planned start. And she made the best of it. If the picture was a failure, Myrna wasn't. Other studios heard about her and her exotic charm. They wanted her for their pictures. Almost over night, she was in demand.

In Exotic Roles

She was always given an oriental, or exotic part. She was Chinese, Javanese, Japanese, Hindu, Gypsy and Egyptian in one picture after the other. That was all right at the start. She changed her name from Williams to Loy and affected long lashes, slanting eyebrows. Every movement of her body had that sensitive swing. Her clothes had a touch of the mysterious Far East. It was rumored that she was a

half caste. Tutored by seasoned experts in the line of publicity, she said nothing. And the less she said, the more the wags believed the concoctions of their own minds.

Success, like the distances between planets, is all a matter of relativity. When she was kicking and skipping in Grauman's Egyptian Theatre chorus, she would have thought her success as an exotic portrayer of oriental roles the very top in accomplishment. Now it was different. It seemed so easy and so natural. She looked to the even higher stratas of film recognition. She was now only a featured player. She wanted star billing and she made up her mind she would get it.

Myrna argued with producers, directors, casting directors and other executives. She tried to tell them she had dramatic talents. But, no, she was too valuable as the half-caste. They kept putting her off, dodging the issue. Myrna Loy wouldn't let them dodge it. She was determined.

Concentrated on Career

And what about her private life? Early in the struggle, Myrna Loy realized that it would be a hard enough struggle if she concentrated on her career. She realized that love affairs would be an encumbrance. Being more of an artistically minded person, she didn't mind missing the night life of Hollywood. In books, at the piano, on the tennis court or the bridle paths, she found her relaxation. Once, early in her career, her name was linked with that of Barry Norton. Pursuing her tight-lipped policy, she didn't bother making denials. The rumors died a natural death. Then, when she made *The Barbarian*, it was reported she might marry Ramon Novarro, who shared star honors with her.

Then when she reached the top, right after her success in *The Thin Man*, she met the man she could love. And, having attained her professional goal, having made her mark in life, she let loose the emotional strings. The marriage was something of an elopement, but it wasn't a surprise to Hollywood. She had known Arthur Hornblow, Jr., for three years and for a year before that eventful trip to Ensenada, Mexico, their friends had known, of their deep interest in one another.

It would seem that just as she carved and moulded her highly successful professional career, Myrna Loy has also guided her private life to the ultimately happy and lasting goal—that of contented home and family life.

Their Romance Rocked the
Foundations of an Empire!

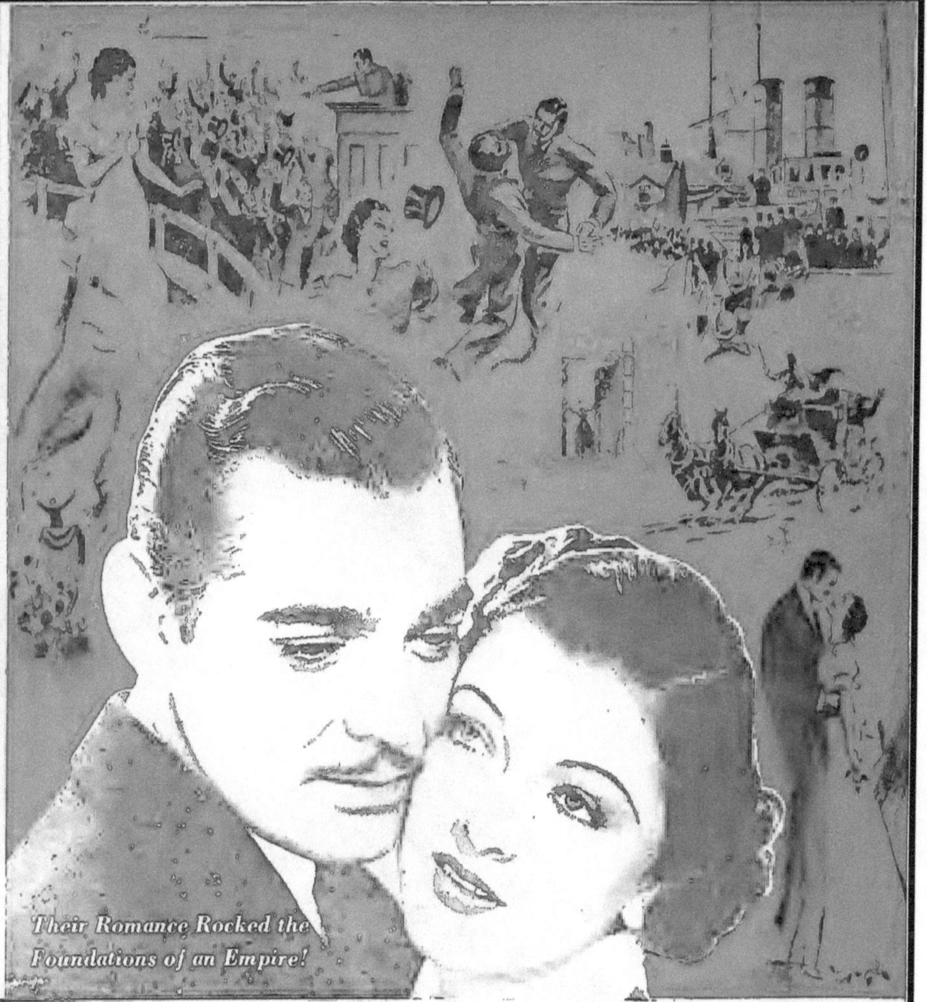

THE MOST *Powerful* LOVE STORY EVER FILMED!
...Of a Patriot Who Lost a Country When He Found a Woman

You thought "San Francisco" was exciting—but wait! You'll be thrilled to your finger-tips when this mighty drama comes thundering from the screen. A fiery romance with your two favorite stars!...CLARK GABLE—courageous, masterful leader of a fighting nation . . ,

MYRNA LOY—the bewitching beauty in whose arms he forgot the pain of leadership . . .

Answering the call of millions of picture-goers M-G-M has brought them together in the most dramatic heart-stabbing love story of our time!

CLARK GABLE · MYRNA LOY
IN
PARNELL

A Metro-Goldwyn-Mayer production based on the great stage play that thrilled Broadway for months, with EDNA MAY OLIVER, BILLIE BURKE, and a great M-G-M cast. Directed and produced by John Stahl.

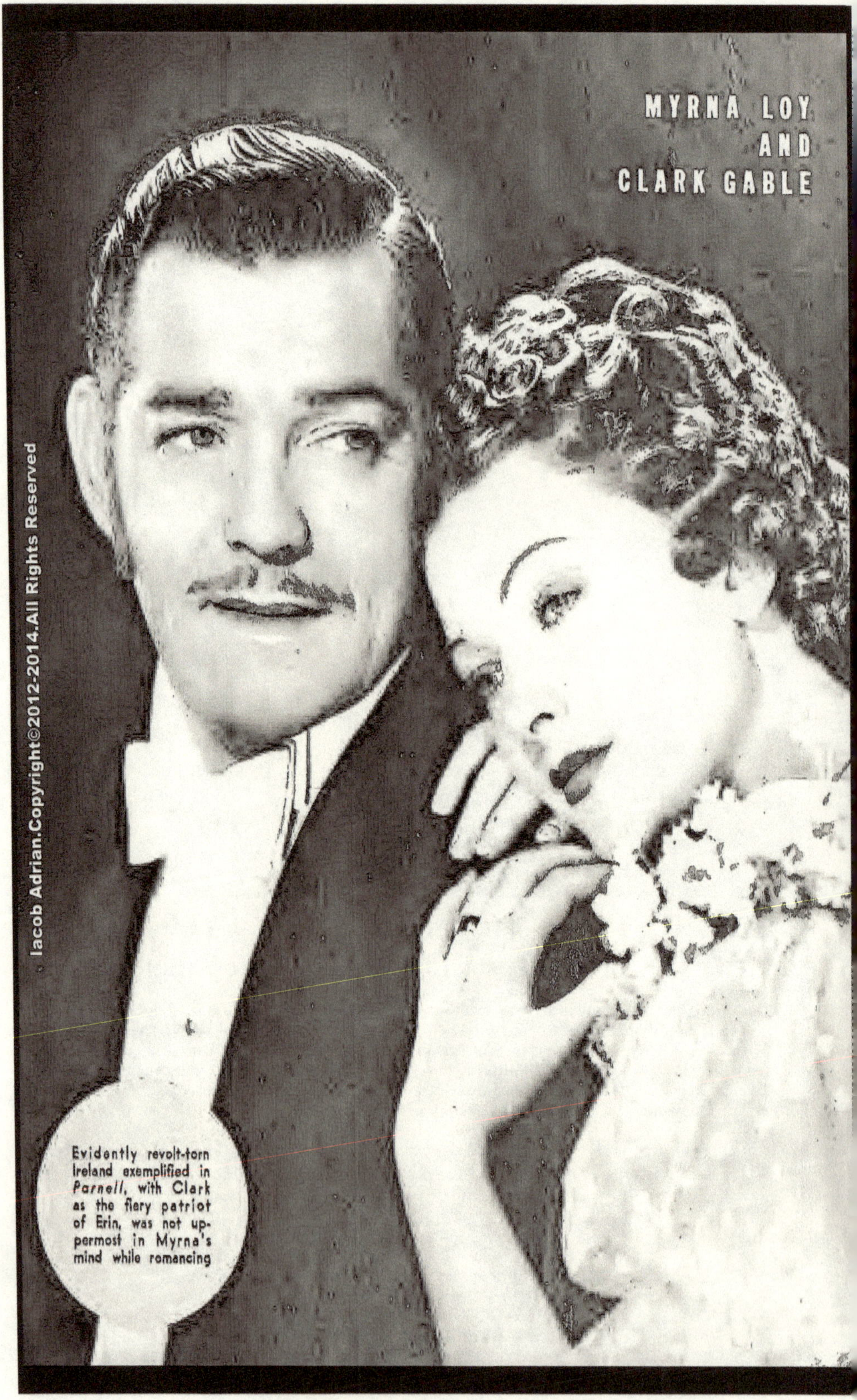

MYRNA LOY
AND
CLARK GABLE

Evidently revolt-torn
Ireland exemplified in
Parnell, with Clark
as the fiery patriot
of Erin, was not up-
permost in Myrna's
mind while romancing

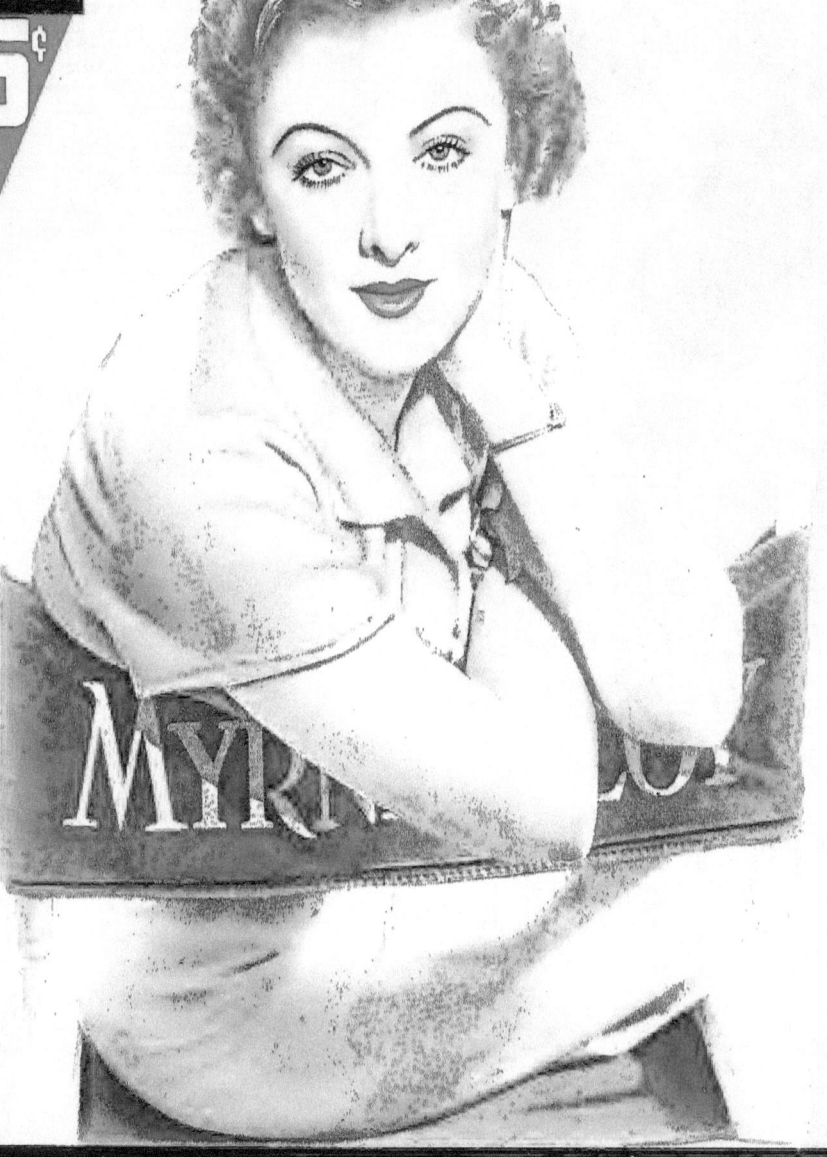

Hollywood

A FAWCETT PUBLICATION

N&C

JUNE

HOLLYWOOD

5¢

MYR

HOW WILL THE GABLE-LOMBARD ROMANCE END?

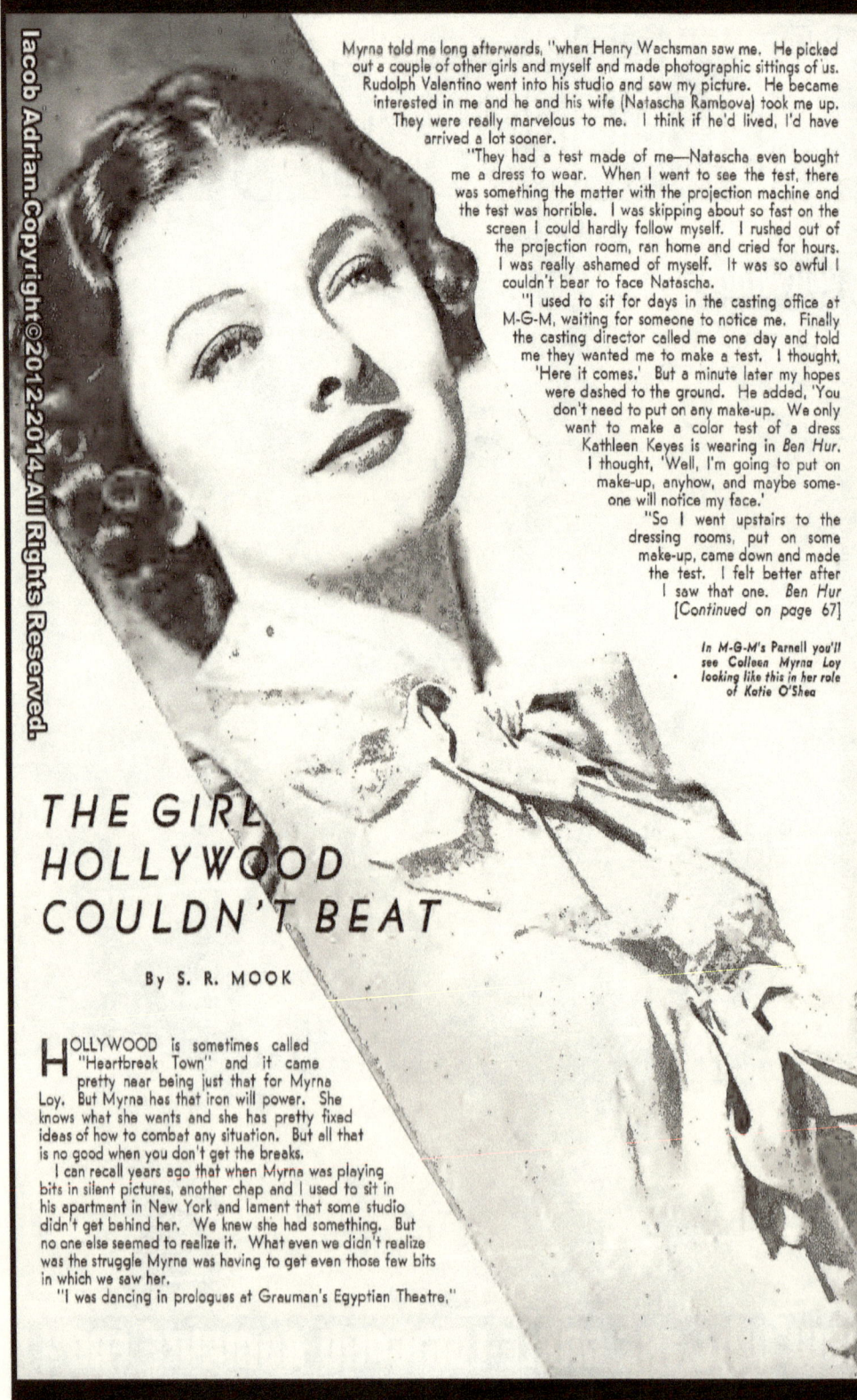

Myrna told me long afterwards, "when Henry Wachsman saw me. He picked out a couple of other girls and myself and made photographic sittings of us. Rudolph Valentino went into his studio and saw my picture. He became interested in me and he and his wife (Natascha Rambova) took me up. They were really marvelous to me. I think if he'd lived, I'd have arrived a lot sooner.

"They had a test made of me—Natascha even bought me a dress to wear. When I went to see the test, there was something the matter with the projection machine and the test was horrible. I was skipping about so fast on the screen I could hardly follow myself. I rushed out of the projection room, ran home and cried for hours. I was really ashamed of myself. It was so awful I couldn't bear to face Natascha.

"I used to sit for days in the casting office at M-G-M, waiting for someone to notice me. Finally the casting director called me one day and told me they wanted me to make a test. I thought, 'Here it comes.' But a minute later my hopes were dashed to the ground. He added, 'You don't need to put on any make-up. We only want to make a color test of a dress Kathleen Keyes is wearing in *Ben Hur*. I thought, 'Well, I'm going to put on make-up, anyhow, and maybe someone will notice my face.'

"So I went upstairs to the dressing rooms, put on some make-up, came down and made the test. I felt better after I saw that one. *Ben Hur* [Continued on page 67]

In M-G-M's Parnell you'll see Colleen Myrna Loy looking like this in her role of Katie O'Shea

THE GIRL HOLLYWOOD COULDN'T BEAT

By S. R. MOOK

HOLLYWOOD is sometimes called "Heartbreak Town" and it came pretty near being just that for Myrna Loy. But Myrna has that iron will power. She knows what she wants and she has pretty fixed ideas of how to combat any situation. But all that is no good when you don't get the breaks.

I can recall years ago that when Myrna was playing bits in silent pictures, another chap and I used to sit in his apartment in New York and lament that some studio didn't get behind her. We knew she had something. But no one else seemed to realize it. What even we didn't realize was the struggle Myrna was having to get even those few bits in which we saw her.

"I was dancing in prologues at Grauman's Egyptian Theatre,"

The Girl Hollywood Couldn't Beat

was so far behind schedule by that time they had divided it up into units. Christie Cabanne was in charge of one unit. He saw the test and did notice my face. Immediately he wanted me for the part of the Madonna in the picture.

"But there were two factions in the studio. One faction wanted a name and the other faction thought the Madonna shouldn't be sullied with a Hollywood reputation. Christie finally won out. He came to me one morning and said, 'It's all set. You're a cinch. The only possible thing that can happen is they want Betty Bronson. She's only played *Peter Pan* so her reputation wouldn't hurt the Madonna. But I know they can't get her.'

"At noon he came back from lunch looking pretty glum. He told me they'd got Bronson. Can you realize what that meant to me? To have an important part in a picture like that practically in my clutches and then lose it?

"I was so broken-hearted I went back to Natascha. It was the first time I'd phoned her or seen her since my first test. She'd seen the test in the meantime and told me it wasn't bad—that it must have been the projection machine that made it seem so. She gave me the lead in a picture she was producing herself. It was a bad picture and never got a first run release. But it served its purpose—so far as I was concerned. Someone at Warner Bros. saw it and they signed me for a part in a picture called *Satan in Sables* starring Lowell Sherman. There were about sixteen women in his life in that picture. I was the trollop who lured him to parties, broke champagne glasses and was a hellcat in general. I got a kick out of doing it..

"My part ran about ten days but after the third day of shooting they came to me and signed me up on a contract, and I was off on a long career of heavies."

"Did you know they were only going to use you for that kind of part?" I asked.

"Heavens, no," she laughed. "All I knew was I was under contract to a big studio and I thought I was going to be a big star."

"Didn't you ever come close to getting a big part out there?" I demanded.

MYRNA shook her head at me pityingly. "Things didn't happen that way then. There were lots of parts I wanted to play but they were all for the Patsy Ruth Millers and May McAvoys. Stars were that type then."

That was something else this other chap and I didn't know. All we knew was Myrna was under contract to a major studio and we shook hands on it. Myrna was on her way. She played the Oriental dancer in *The Desert Song* —her first talkie—and made a big hit. But nothing happened. She went right on playing Oriental heavies. At the end of four and a half years they let her option lapse.

"Fired me," says Myrna bluntly. "Do you know, I even had to make up my own dialects in those early talkies. Scenario writers never even attempted to write dialect into their scripts and there was no one in Hollywood at the time who made even a pretense of teaching you an authentic dialect. I used to make it up, recite the speeches aloud and think, 'Now, that doesn't sound bad.' "

Fox signed her shortly afterwards for a part in *Renegade* with Warner Baxter. She played another heavy. But before the picture was completed they had signed her to a contract. At the end of a year they let her go.

The only comforting part of that year's work (aside from the regular salary which, in those days, was not large) was the fact that William K. Howard cast her as the loyal little wife in *Transatlantic*. It was Myrna's first American part. Everyone advised Bill against it but he stood adamant and was rewarded with a fine portrayal by Myrna.

When Fox failed to take up her option she went to her agents, Minna Wallis and Ruth Collier. "Myrna," they chorused, "you've got to break away from these Oriental parts. You'll just have to take anything we can get for you until we can establish you as an American."

"Suits me," the girl from Montana acquiesced.

SO FOR a couple of years more she appeared in bits—and I mean bits. But they were Caucasians. She appeared with Ronald Colman in *Arrowsmith* and *Devil to Pay*. Arthur Hornblow, the gentleman who is now her husband, cast her as an American whenever he had a part in one of his pictures for her.

Then M-G-M signed her. Instead of rejoicing, she went into a blue funk. They specialize in women stars. That was the trouble. They had Garbo, Crawford, Shearer and Harlow. Any part that came up would fit one or the other of them. Myrna would get what was left or what they wouldn't do.

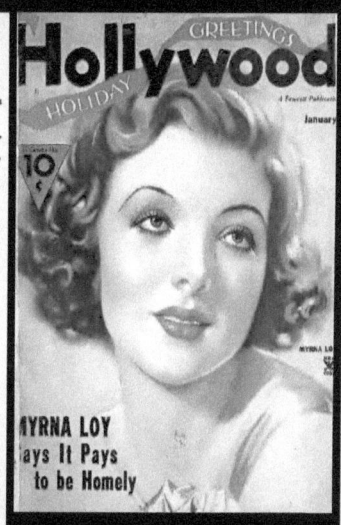

HOLLYWOOD
GREETINGS
HOLIDAY
January
10¢

MYRNA LOY
Says It Pays
to be Homely

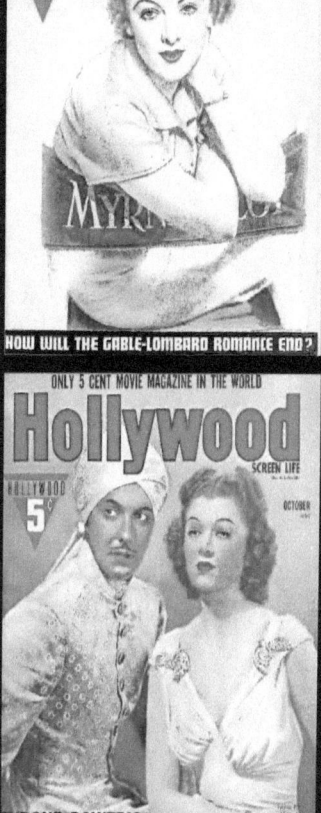

Hollywood
JUNE
5¢

MYRNA LOY

HOW WILL THE GABLE-LOMBARD ROMANCE END?

ONLY 5 CENT MOVIE MAGAZINE IN THE WORLD

Hollywood
SCREEN LIFE
OCTOBER
5¢

TYRONE POWER'S
MOST DARING ROLE!

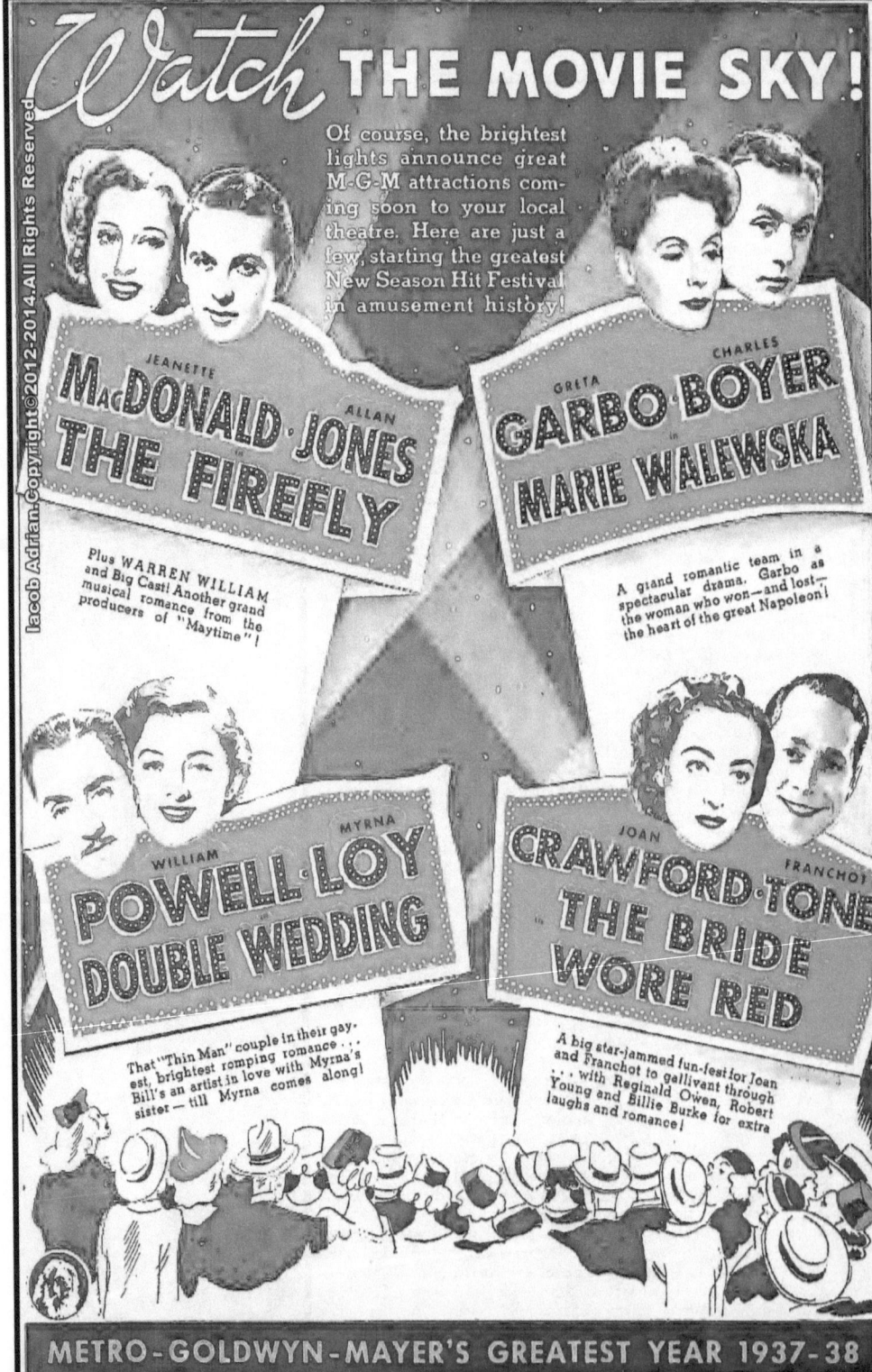

Watch THE MOVIE SKY!

Of course, the brightest lights announce great M-G-M attractions coming soon to your local theatre. Here are just a few, starting the greatest New Season Hit Festival in amusement history!

JEANETTE
MacDONALD · JONES ALLAN
THE FIREFLY

GRETA CHARLES
GARBO · BOYER
MARIE WALEWSKA

Plus WARREN WILLIAM and Big Cast! Another grand musical romance from the producers of "Maytime"!

A grand romantic team in a spectacular drama. Garbo as the woman who won—and lost—the heart of the great Napoleon!

WILLIAM MYRNA
POWELL · LOY
DOUBLE WEDDING

JOAN FRANCHOT
CRAWFORD · TONE
THE BRIDE WORE RED

That "Thin Man" couple in their gayest, brightest romping romance . . . Bill's an artist in love with Myrna's sister — till Myrna comes along!

A big star-jammed fun-fest for Joan and Franchot to gallivant through . . . with Reginald Owen, Robert Young and Billie Burke for extra laughs and romance!

METRO-GOLDWYN-MAYER'S GREATEST YEAR 1937-38

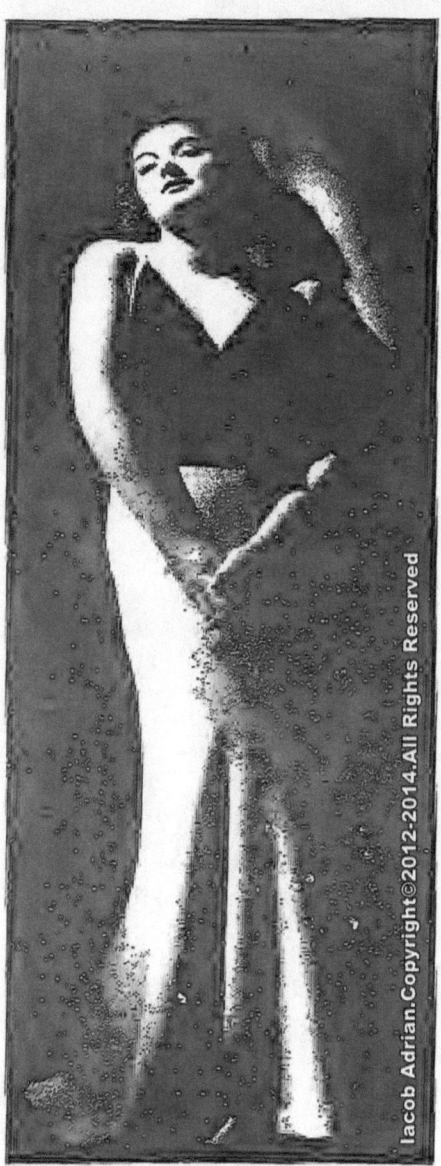

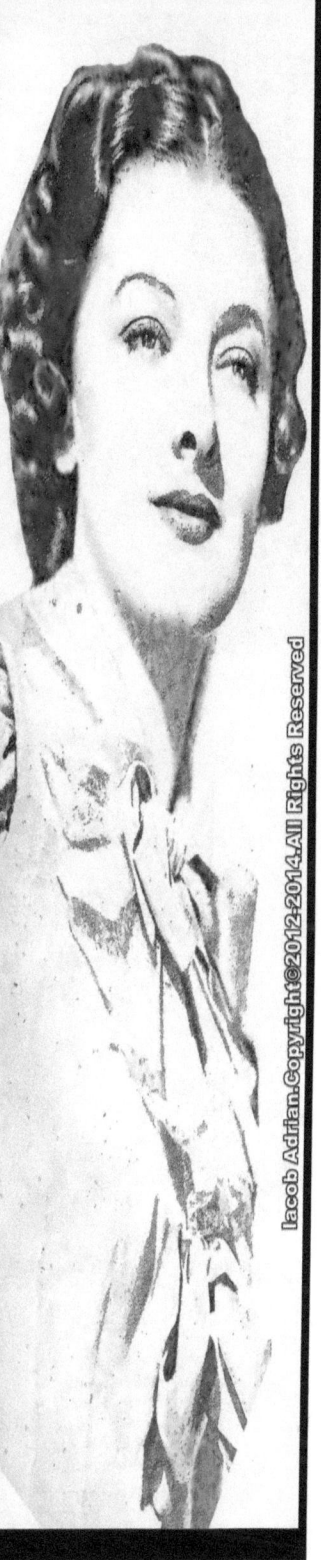

NEXT MONTH

Lovely Myrna Loy makes the startling statement, "It Takes Three To Make a Love Affair" and argues the point in one of the most provocative feature stories ever to come out of Hollywood.

DON'T MISS IT!

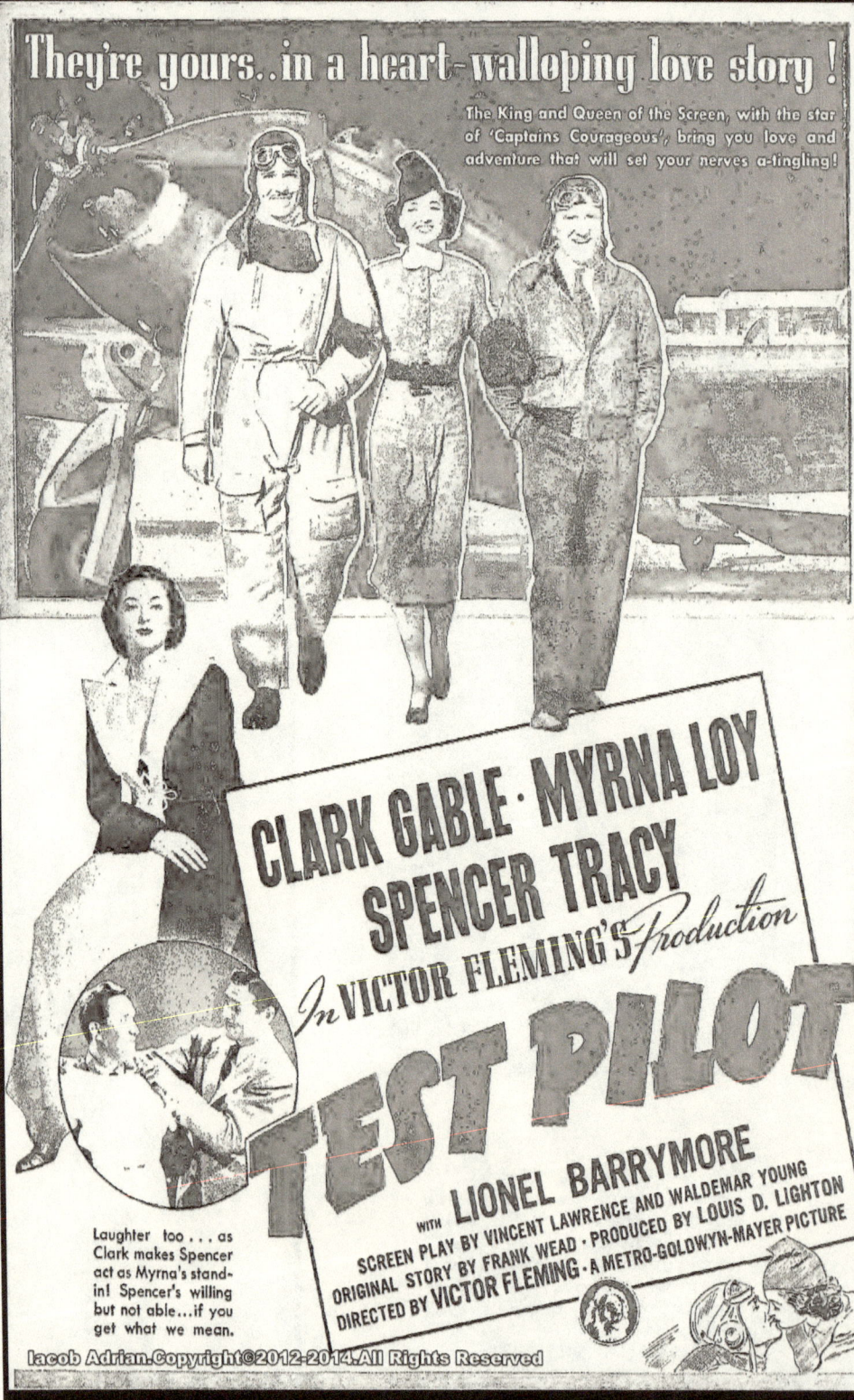

They're yours..in a heart-walloping love story!

The King and Queen of the Screen, with the star of 'Captains Courageous', bring you love and adventure that will set your nerves a-tingling!

CLARK GABLE · MYRNA LOY
SPENCER TRACY
In VICTOR FLEMING's Production
TEST PILOT

LIONEL BARRYMORE
WITH
SCREEN PLAY BY VINCENT LAWRENCE AND WALDEMAR YOUNG
ORIGINAL STORY BY FRANK WEAD · PRODUCED BY LOUIS D. LIGHTON
DIRECTED BY VICTOR FLEMING · A METRO-GOLDWYN-MAYER PICTURE

Laughter too . . . as Clark makes Spencer act as Myrna's stand-in! Spencer's willing but not able...if you get what we mean.

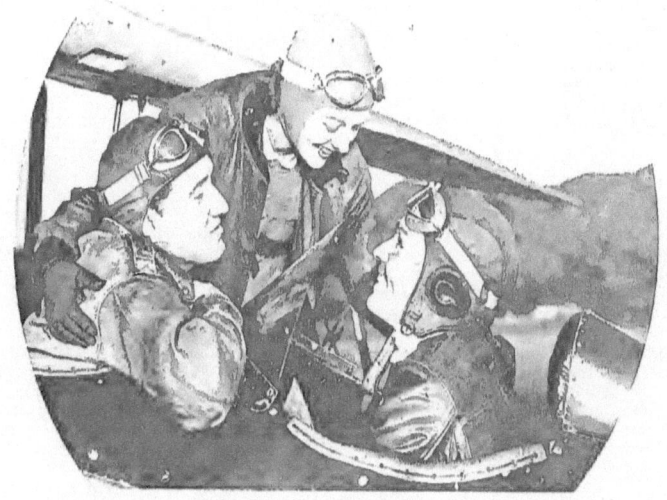

IT TAKES THREE TO MAKE A LOVE AFFAIR

Above are the three who make the love affair in *Test Pilot*, soon to be released

■ "It takes three," remarked Myrna Loy, "to make a love affair."

She tipped her pretty auburn head upward in the captivating Loy manner and let a quizzical sparkle slide into her gray-green eyes. Yet she meant what she said. Her tone was serious.

"When a girl isn't truly in love with John Doe, she finds that out after meeting John Roe," said Myrna, "but when a girl's truly in love with John Doe, even a temporary infatuation for John Roe only makes her realize how much she loves the first one. I've watched it work out in the case of some acquaintances. Not that I recommend the method—it's too chancey!

"Just the same, a modern woman ought to look twice before she leaps—into matrimony. Oh, it certainly takes three to make a love affair; the third one's for comparison, for making up her mind. Rather often he turns out to be the man she marries after all."

It is from the dilemmas and tribulations of a large circle of friends that Myrna has deduced the need of a third party to the average courtship and from her observations she has drawn a number of shrewd conclusions. She smiled, recalled them, as she lounged in her buff and green dressing room at the M-G-M studios.

Everybody has heard about the course of true love seldom running smoothly, but Myrna Loy introduces a note of reassurance, by saying that rough going is all to the good in the happy ending

By
JESSIE HENDERSON

That girl with a temporary infatuation for John Roe, of whom Myrna had spoken, went absolutely haywire for a month over this handsome stranger who cut in at a dance on her fiancé, John Doe. Still engaged to Doe, she dashed around with the new lad like one bewitched while the whole town, diverted and scandalized, argued as to the outcome. She swam with the new heart interest, rode with him, gazed earnestly into his dark eyes, even tried to learn to cook his favorite dishes ("An almost fatal symptom!" Myrna commented.), until, all of a sudden—pfft! She realized in a flash that this wasn't the real thing and galloped madly back to her first love. They've been happily married

now for five years. The point is, she might never have married Doe, at least she probably wouldn't have settled down to a contented wedded life with him, except that by comparing him with the scintillant Roe she discovered the difference. Roe's glitter was tinsel and Doe's quieter gleam was pure gold.

Wise, and sweet, is the philosophy Myrna has evolved from the things she's seen others do along these lines, or neglect to do. That aristocratic, somewhat Mona Lisa smile of hers, deepened at various recollections. Cool and poised as she always seems to be—cooler than ever in the smart green tweed frock—her strongest characteristic is nevertheless a keen sense of humor. She says you need a sense of humor most when you have it least; that is, when you're in love.

"Comparison!" she insisted, "not jealousy!"

In other words, she went on to explain, if the man you love goes out with another girl, don't grow jealous. Instead, remind yourself: "Well, I compare favorably with her," and see to it that you do compare favorably with her by not flying into a tantrum. This getting jealous is a lack of self respect, an inferiority complex.

But if you can't help feeling jealous, in other words if

It Takes Three to Make a Love Affair

you insist on considering yourself less alluring than the girl he's taken out for an evening, at least don't be catty. Myrna doesn't believe in catty-ness under any circumstances. "Be bigger than the situation," she advised with a sage wag of that auburn head, "or else you give him the chance to say, 'Ho, ho, I was right. The second girl *is* nicer.'"

In a three-cornered crisis of this sort, she proceeded, when the man of your heart shows a right interest in somebody else, the big thing is not to make any phony gestures. For instance, don't say, "She's such a dear; too bad she's bowlegged." A man—yes, even a man—catches on to that kind of sabotage after a while. No, the thing to do is to do nothing. This is one of the hardest things in the world to do, and one of the most effective. Take competition as a challenge. Perhaps the other girl is nice, and it's up to you to be nicer. Anyhow, in getting jealous you simply hurt yourself and oftener than not help your rival.

A mousey, diffident little girl whom Myrna knew about went into a fury of despair and indignation because her boy friend took another girl to a dance. Admittedly, it was a rather funny thing for him to do, but he did it. Feeling that right was on her side, she wasted no time when she met him on the street next day but immediately plunged into a hot argument during which her voice grew louder and higher. All mouseyness, all diffidence, fled.

She embarrassed the man. As she saw people pause in astonishment, she embarrassed herself. Abruptly she stopped in mid sentence, but too late. "There!" she snapped angrily, on a more subdued note, "I've never made a scene in public before. It's all your fault—I hope that'll teach you *something*."

"It's taught me several things," replied the man who had first admired her for her appealing little-mouse quality. Among other things it taught him that, as his wife, the girl might unexpectedly make him ridiculous in public or miserable in private. He dropped her as if she'd been a hot brick.

No, even under the most trying circumstances of this kind, the thing to do (Myrna was repeating) is to do nothing. And if you're very, very clever, you not only do nothing; you say nothing. That's the hardest, and cleverest move of all. Let the one who has made the mistake and gone away be the first to come back. For, look: If the situation doesn't eventually smooth out, then—since the erring one's affection wasn't any stronger than that—it's a good thing the break came when it did. Under those conditions, it couldn't come too soon.

"When such a situation arises," Myrna added, "when the man begins taking another girl around, the strain generally

brings out the first girl's worst qualities. At the very time when she should be at her best! She ought to put the situation in the bottom drawer and leave it there till the whole thing's finished, one way or another; not keep dragging it forth to display to her friends or to weep over in secret."

You must take these things, Myrna believes, philosophically. Though you don't realize it at the time, it is probably nature's way of working things out. Often the damsel who wept and wailed over her delinquent boy friend has found—rather promptly, too—another boy with whom she could be happier than she'd ever have been with the first.

Take, for example, the maiden who languished because the man of her choice ever so often fell in love with a new face. Fundamentally, he assured her, he didn't absolutely love any of these lesser flames but he hated to be tied down to one girl friend all the time. The maiden reasoned, and her reasoning was good, that if he cared a lot about her he wouldn't flitter here and there with others; even if he did come back to her when the new interests began to pall.

One evening, abandoned in somewhat cavalier manner at a night club for a long hour while the gay Lothario tentatively flirted with a new blonde on the terrace, the maiden suddenly murmured an excuse to the rest of the party, wrapped her cloak about her shoulders, and marched to the door to summon a taxi. She was going home. She was through. But at the doorway she ran plump into a young man so mad he gibbered when he tried to speak. She recognized him as the erstwhile escort of her own Lothario's new blonde. Misery loves company. The two jilted ones joined forces, adjourned to another night club to discuss their grievances, and found that they both liked the old-fashioned waltz and roast wienies.

They both liked dependability, too. Consequently, each was dependable. Therefore they married each other. But in each case it had taken a third person to help on the decision.

This anecdote has a sequel. The dependable one didn't roam from his own fireside, but he had a temper. Still, his wife had a sense of humor. One breakfast he grew so annoyed about a telephone message from the office that he threw his (empty) coffee cup across the room. Not at his wife, but at the wall.

Did friend wife rush out to see her lawyer? Not she; for, as Myrna points out, love—when you come down to brass tacks —can stand practically anything but disloyalty. If more wives—and husbands—would remember this and summon a sense of humor before an emergency grew into a crash, there'd be fewer decisions in Reno.

When the husband stamped out of the house, so mad he forgot the goodbye kiss, this wife didn't feel that All Was Over. She collected the coffee cup. That evening at dinner when she brought in the coffee pot she put a gleaming china cup at her

own place and a jagged fragment of hubby's morning coffee cup, balanced delicately upon a saucer, at his. Hubby burst out laughing, and the incident was closed.

Myrna thought this coffee cup diplomacy was about the best she'd ever heard. For Myrna, despite her pronounced femininity—notice those little hands making graceful gestures while she talks—has a man's viewpoint, and that's a rare thing in woman. She knows, for illustration, how to drop small discussions, small plans, small differences of opinion, without making a fuss about them; knows this better than any other woman I've ever met. It takes a matter of major importance to make her grow serious to the extent of insistence. And, incidentally, when she does battle for a thing she considers important she does so with calmness and good taste.

In short, Myrna's convinced that the great life-saver for engagements, and for marriages, is appreciation of what you have. Don't get so used to love that you slight it. Getting used to love and slighting it is why marriages have a "ten-year lull," why they slump into the commonplace within ten years, and often sooner. The girl who went into an ecstasy of appreciation when her fiance brought half a dozen roses is the same girl who doesn't even say, "Thank you" when the same man after ten years of marriage lets her put a fur coat on the charge account for which he foots the bills. On the other hand, the fiance who brought roses may be the same man who never dreams of bringing home even a bunch of dandelions now. It works both ways.

"A man likes the little, sweet attentions," Myrna said, "the things you did that made him think you were sweet when you first met him; the things that attracted him at the beginning. Keep them up!"

It's a couple of days before the wedding. Your fiance drops by to remark modestly: "I went around the course in 80 today." You leap to your feet, palpitant with admiration, kiss him soundly, and exclaim in accents of awed enthusiasm: "Dar-ling! How won-derful!!"

Oh, sweet little woman! Who wouldn't marry you, y.u pet?

Okay. It's ten years later. Husband comes home, beaming. "I broke 80 today," he brags. You're reading a book. "So what?" you snap. All right, all right, Sourpuss; but if this were ten years ago there wouldn't have been any wedding bells.

Well, that same evening, while you're dining with friends, your husband says to their house guest. "I broke 80 today." "Really?" she squeals. "How wonderful!!"

And pretty soon your friends begin to hint how your husband and that redheaded snip appear to get along very nicely together and so on and so on and so on. It takes three to show two where they stand.

See? See what Myrna means?

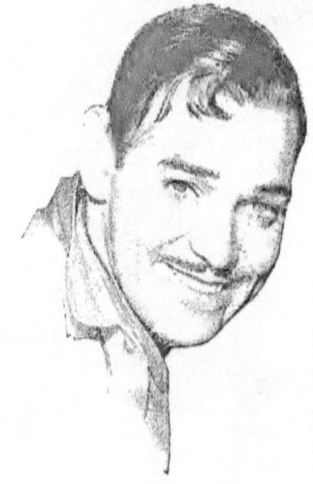

CLARK GABLE

"TOO HOT TO HANDLE"

MYRNA LOY

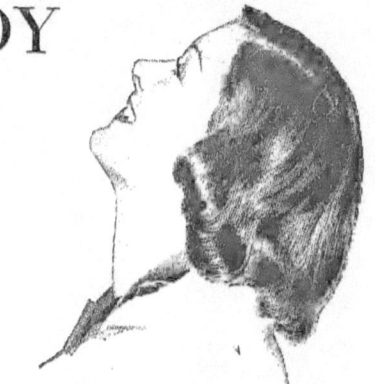

The best news since "Test Pilot" with that rare pair of romancers, M·G·M's tantalizing twosome. Clark's a daredevil newsreel man—Myrna's an airdevil aviatrix...Action! Heart-pumping paradise for thrill and fun-loving picture fans!

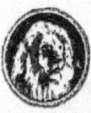

with WALTER PIDGEON · WALTER CONNOLLY LEO CARRILLO · Screen Play by John Lee Mahin and Laurence Stallings Directed by Jack Conway · Produced by Lawrence Weingarten · A Metro-Goldwyn-Mayer Picture

Side-Tracked
Siren

Just exactly what is the new style in sirens? Myrna Loy, who made a specialty of the slinking walk, the secret smile, the narrowed eyes of the vamp of yesterday, tells you what to expect of the 1939 siren

By KAY PROCTOR

This is a story about Wicked Women, 1939 style. Because—

The Side-tracked Siren is in the groove again. Once more the erstwhile "Perfect Wife" of the screen, Myrna Loy, is going on the vampage.

Secretly, Myrna is pretty set-up about it all; she has found, I imagine, that perfection is not all it is cracked up to be. She admits, however, that when she was cast as the strong-willed temptress, Lady Esketh, in the forthcoming picturiza-

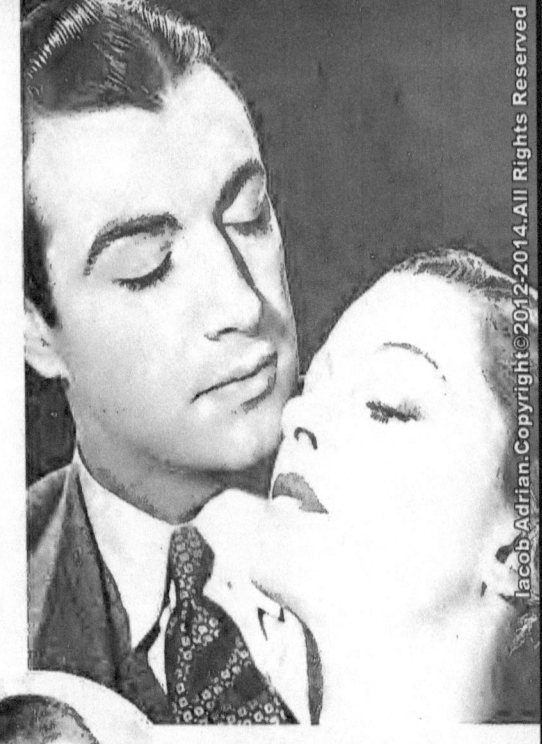

Above, Robert Taylor looks with respect and pleasure, too, at the 1939 siren in *Lucky Night*

This is the way Myrna Loy played the woman of dangerous allure in *The Mask of Fu Manchu*, one of her first vamps

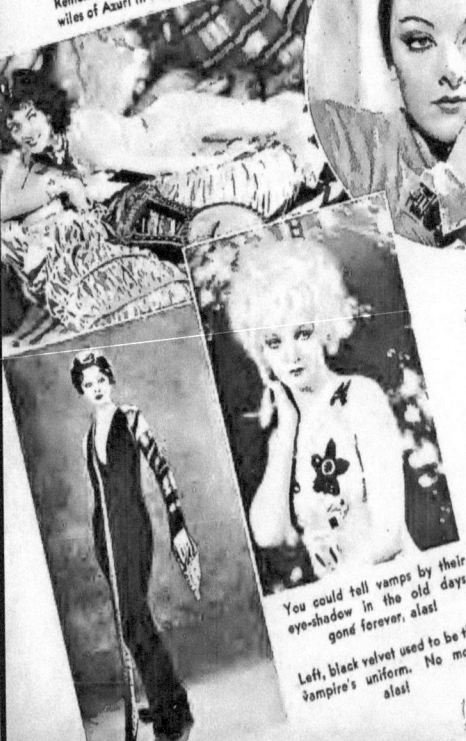

Remember the simple, if sinful, wiles of Azuri in *The Desert Song?*

You could tell vamps by their eye-shadow in the old days, gone forever, alas!

Left, black velvet used to be the vampire's uniform. No more, alas!

tion of the best seller novel, *The Rains Came*, she was a little shocked.

"Frankly I was taken aback at the idea," she laughed. "I'd got so in the mental habit of 'nice girl' parts that a siren seemed, well unthinkable. Me a Wicked Woman? Perish the thought! My sireny belonged to the dear, dead past."

Then, she said, she realized it might be fun because sireny 'ain't what it used to be,' and the passing of years has stream-lined it into a pretty nifty model of behavior. Neat but not gaudy.

You remember the screen sirens of yesteryear. "Vamps" we called them. Slinky creatures they were with their lamp-blacked eyes, usually taped into an oriental slant; lacquered hair, always midnight black and coiffed to spell menace; and dead-white pans with exaggerated lips which were supposed to convey the idea of voluptuous and irresistible appeal. They slithered around in flowing draperies that would give the Hays Office a nightmare today, and stretched themselves out on fur bedecked couches to clasp The Hero to their ample bosoms in long, ardent (and how!) embrace. They had two facial expressions: a dirty leer, which meant they were up to no good; and passion, which usually turned out the same way.

For some strange reason, they always seemed very sad about their work, judging by their dolorous mien, which subtly suggested the life of a siren wasn't any great shakes when you came right down to it. Maybe it was because they always got their come-uppance in the end.

First, last and always, they

Side-Tracked Siren

were what used to be so quaintly called "A Fallen Woman." Social pariahs, they were; outcasts ostracized by one and all. They were Sin with a capital S, because Sin and Sex were synonymous.

You remember them—Theda Bara, Nita Naldi, Barbara LaMarr, Pola Negri, Rosemary Theby, Olga Baclanova, Merle Oberon and a young lady named Myrna Loy. Or maybe you've forgotten a little dilly called *The Mask of Fu Manchu* in which she aided and abetted Boris Karloff in some dark villainy, or *Satan in Sables* in which she played Lowell Sherman's extra-legal heart interest of the moment? Myrna hasn't forgotten.

Myrna first became a siren by an out-and-out fluke; it was a toss-up between two parts—a mistress and a madonna. She often has wondered what would have happened if the breaks had been the other way. It started when Rudolph Valentino and his wife, Natacha Rambova, saw Myrna dancing in a Grauman prologue and were struck by her piquant beauty. They made a straight screen test of her, but nothing came of it. Some time later M-G-M made another test of her, this time for the role of the Madonna in the great spectacle *Ben Hur*. For four hours she actually had the role, since it was deemed fitting that an unknown actress should play the reverent role. Then the

Box-office Boys began yelling for a Name, and Betty Bronson was given the part.

The Valentinos refused to give up their faith in Myrna. Natacha, who was an exotic person herself and a designer of some renown, one day gave way to a flight of fancy. She dressed Myrna up in a bizarre costume of her own designing, painted an extreme make-up upon the frankly American features of the Loy face, and set a sleek black wig upon the Loy head. The effect was startling. It was a complete transformation. Warner Brothers saw a photograph and promptly cast her for the mistress bit in *Satan in Sables*. That led to a five year contract during which time she played more sirens than she can remember, including the dusky charmer in *The Desert Song*.

Curiously, too, her last siren part was also her first wife role, albeit the wife was of a different breed from what she has been portraying since. It was in that sophisticated picture, *The Animal Kingdom* in which Myrna was the wife who was a heartless, selfish, scheming minx and Ann Harding, as the mistress of Leslie Howard, was the soul of understanding, generosity and nobility itself.

"I think that picture really presaged the change in sirens," Myrna said. "For the first time 'the other woman' was not a 'bad' woman. She, in fact, was endowed

with the qualities and virtues theretofore strictly reserved for the women living safely within the bounds of holy matrimony. It gave people something to think about."

Had that attitude not been accurately and honestly reflected in the changing social conditions in the world, no producer ever would have dared to so present it on the screen, Myrna went on.

"It is true that in some things like fashions, make-up, little fads and perhaps even architecture and decoration, life copies from the screen," she said. "But in all major issues, such as social standards, the screen copies from life. Therefore the pattern for our modern screen sirens comes straight from a convincing counterpart in real life."

By the same token, it would be silly to pretend that the old-fashioned "vamps" of the movies accurately reflected the real life sirens of yesteryear, Myrna continued. They were ridiculous in the exaggeration of their lack of virtue. Any similarity to any person, living or dead, wasn't coincidental, it was darned near impossible! But just as "nice" women never openly admitted the existence of less fortunate or more fascinating sisters, so the screen took it upon itself always to teach an impressive moral lesson by painting them much blacker than necessity or fact warranted. Perforce she wore her stripes for all to see.

"The modern siren doesn't wear any stripes," she said. "In the first place, she's

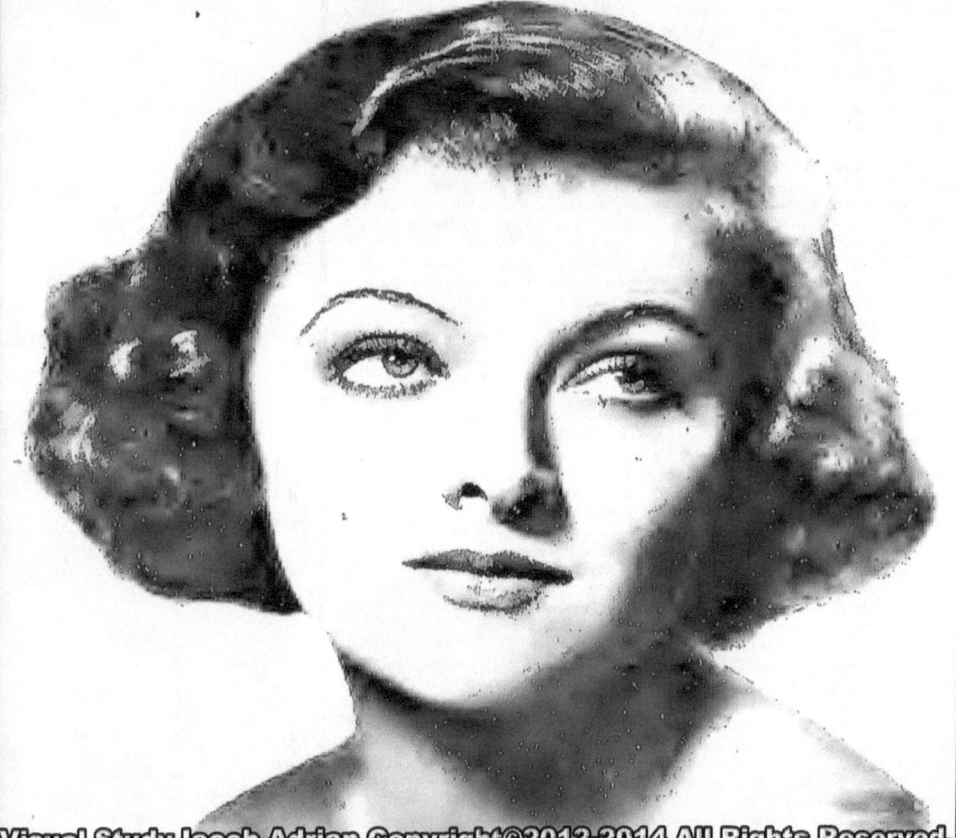

usually far too clever for that, and in the second place, the chances are she has no stripes to wear. The term 'Siren' no longer implies a lack of morals; in many cases it is the happily married wife who is the siren so far as her husband is concerned. She is the one who spells allure, glamour and mystery to him, and rightly so. The change in social standards, customs and conditions since the inhibited Victorian era has made it possible."

The freedom in behavior now permitted well-bred women is the keynote of the change, Myrna believes. Once respectability attended church socials, stiff concerts, stuffy teas and musicales, with an occasional cotillion or ball for joint activities of nice women and decent men. Otherwise women sat home with their tatting, or an exciting session with the stereopticon machine showing polite views of Niagara Falls and The Leaning Tower of Pisa. Their men meanwhile were at the club or "out with the boys"—and too frequently, some of "the girls."

Today "nice" women (and happier ones) may join the men in a night club or at a cocktail bar, at a slightly spicy musical comedy, a hot political rally, or even at a poker table where the clatter of chips may go on until the wee hours of the morning and tall steins of beer top off the session. And Mrs. Grundy never bats an eye. It's the thing to do.

"Seems to me it boils down to this," Myrna said. "For some strange reason, custom did not permit a nice woman to be gay. It was unthinkable that she play with her husband and share his good times. Therefore 'the other woman' spelled fun to men. Now social custom no longer stacks the cards in favor of the siren. Wives are playing the same game and giving their erstwhile competitors a good stiff run for their money. Sirens, in fact, have to step lively to keep up with them."

■ The modern siren is quite a complex person, according to Myrna. She has to be. (We're speaking of the threat-to-marital-happiness type now.) Granted that her chief lure is still sex dressed up in less flagrant style, she cannot depend upon it alone. And she knows it.

"A hypothetical modern maid who lures men to their destruction is, of course, a sophisticate who knows all the answers but rarely tells them. She is apt to be restless and concerned with the physical and material side of life. Usually she is rather honest about herself. Beauty is an asset but not a necessity. She wears chic clothes well, often preferring quieter garb than her less predatory sisters. As a rule she is proficient at sports but is careful not to excel.

"Certainly she is more intelligent than in the past," Myrna stated. "Again, she has to be, because nowadays she mingles on an even basis with an educated and cultured society that once upon a time would have refused, point blank, to accept her. If she acts like a lady, she is accepted as one pro tem. Where society once took the attitude of 'Your private affairs are also my business and I don't approve of them,' it now says 'Your morals are your

own business, and frankly, I'm not interested.'"

Recognizing this, picture producers are patterning their 1939 sirens from this new model, just as they recognized some time ago that "nice" heroines also could be devastating sirens. Consider what Goldwyn did with Merle Oberon. Consider Bette Davis in *Jezebel*, Dorothy Lamour and Lana Turner. Consider also the change in Dietrich and the newest bombshell in sireny, Hedy Lamarr.

"Hedy really is making it tough for all of us, heroines and sirens alike," Myrna chuckled. "She combines the best features of each. She is something new in glamour —and she's caught us all off guard!"

Which is as pretty a compliment from one actress to another as I've heard in many a moon. What's more, Myrna meant it. There isn't a jealous bone in the girl's body. But when she again tosses her hat into the sireny ring, I'm not sure that Hedy isn't going to find a lot stiffer competition than she's meeting at the moment. And I'm not sure that wives from coast to coast (and Lapland and the South Seas) aren't going to have fresh cause for complaint; they've witnessed their husbands going overboard for "the perfect wife" so heavens knows what will happen when "the perfect wife" turns into "the perfect siren." A revolution, probably.

You see, this playing a siren isn't going to be a one-shot affair for Myrna. Several of them are on the schedule including the naughty Amytis in *The Road to Rome*. She was the gal, you remember, who had to deal with Hannibal, the invader, to save the home town of Rome. The Hays office finally has cleared the way for the picture production of the famous stage play, and none other than Clark Gable is scheduled to play Hannibal. Some fun! Her current picture, *Lucky Night* with Bob Taylor sort of breaks the news gently to the public; she is a captivating minx in that one. The "perfect wife" won't be lost entirely, though; another Thin Man or two will be sandwiched in between. Likewise, *Sea of Grass* with Spence Tracy.

■ "My only objection to the 'perfect wife' sort of thing is that it entails a danger of typing," Myrna said. "Somehow the public became so saturated with the 'perfect wife' publicity in connection with me that I was expected to become the real life spokesman for the screen wives I played. I'm tired of being asked to hand out practical advice on how to win and hold a husband.

"*Fundamentally, all women are sirens.* We may just as well face it: men don't marry women; women marry men! There is more truth than literary brilliance in that passage from Thackeray's *Vanity Fair* in which he says: 'And this I set down as a positive truth. A woman with fair opportunities, and without a positive hump, may marry whom she likes. Only let us be thankful that the darlings are like the beasts of the fields and don't know their own power. They would overcome us entirely if they did.'

"There is just one difference in sirens today," Myrna concluded. "Some work harder at it!"

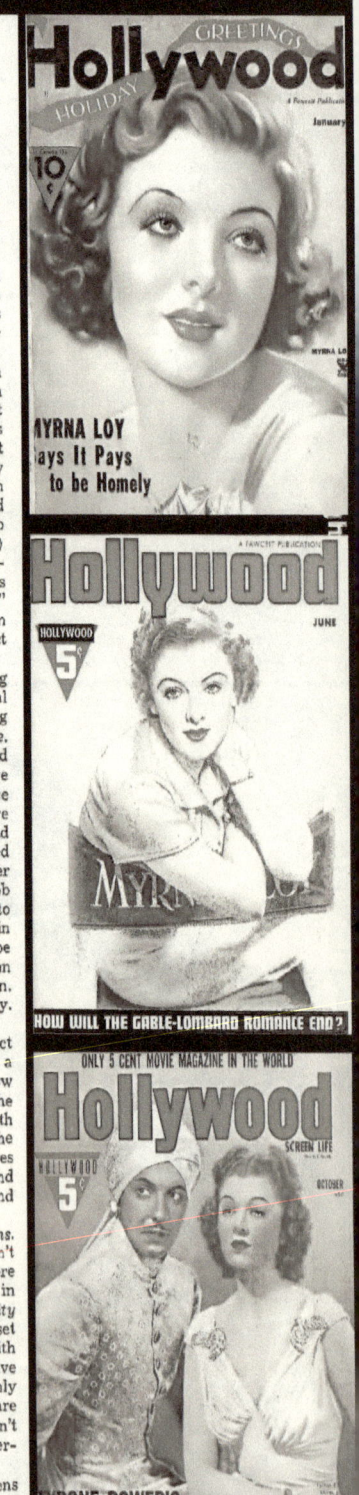

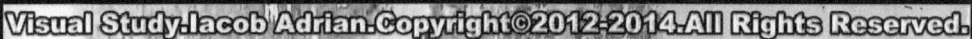

When The Rains Came

Our favorite extra takes time out to sympathize with Noah as he completes his preparations to move to the desert and to lead the life of a camel from now-on

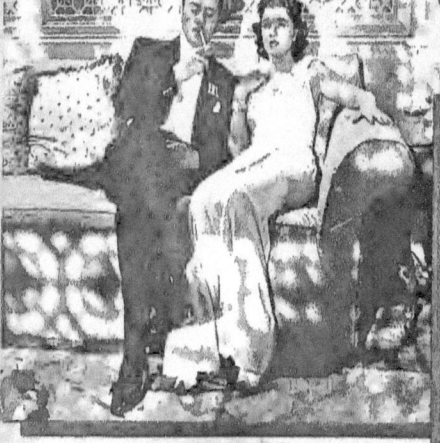

By E. J. (Umbrella Man) SMITHSON

Above, George Brent and Myrna Loy in a scene in the Indian palace before the rains swept the town away. Right, Tyrone Power as an East Indian Major, George Brent, H. B. Warner with little Madame Ouspenskaya

DEAR EDITOR,

Many's the time I've been through hell-and-high-water, got myself stuck on the horns of a dilemma, found myself hiding behind the well-known eight ball, and, in other instances too numerous to mention, found myself running counterclockwise to a safe and sane mode of living. I've always been able to accept these sudden and somewhat erratic departures from orderly and well-established routine without rancor or complaint. In fact I used to welcome and enjoy those jousts as part of the game. If Old Man Fate decided that it was about time to practice up on a mite of buffeting, and went so far as to select me as his sparring partner, I was always Big-hearted Johnnie-on-the-Spot ready, willing and able to square away and swing a couple from my heels whenever an opening presented itself. Fate could dish it out and I could take it, was my motto.

But them days are gone forever. The Old Gent put the finger on me this week, deciding, maybe, that it was time to show me who was boss. And he surely did! I'm not half as tough as I was a week ago. No foolin', going through hell-and-high-water was like a beautiful blonde walking tip-toe through the tulips compared to my going through an earthquake and a flood come Monday, Tuesday, Wednesday, and Thursday of this week.

What deceived me was the innocent beginning of the

When the Rains Came

whole affair. Last Saturday, while I was pressing a fresh crease in my second best pair of pants, The Little Lady who keeps plugging away at the Central Casting switchboard gave me a buzz and says, as impolitely as you please: "Hey, Dopey, hop out to 20th Century-Fox and get yourself an extra job in *The Rains Came*. And listen, big shot, don't think you're going to stand me up tonight like you did a week ago when you asked for a date. I want to eat at eight. 'By."

Well, I obeyed the Little Lady's instructions, and got myself set for four days' work—which I now consider the worst mistake I ever made in my long and troubled life.

How, for instance, was I to know that I was going to be shaken loose from my bridgework by an earthquake the first day when *The Rains Came*—and showered down? How was I to know that after I had recovered (but slightly) from a bad case of the shakes I was to be almost drowned in a flood? Well, believe me, I DIDN'T know! All that I knew about the picture was what I'd been able to decipher from the cast sheet. Myrna Loy, George Brent, Tyrone Power, Joseph Schildkraut, Maria Ouspenskaya, and an 18-year-old newcomer by the name of Brenda Joyce (who is going to be the big surprise of the picture, else I'm no judge of good looks coupled to better acting!) were all listed as principals, and I thought how nice it would be if, a couple of months from now, I could go around boasting that I had played in a picture with them.

Mr. Darryl Zanuck, so further reading disclosed, had paid $52,000 for the screen rights to the Bromfield novel and was laying $2,500,000 smack on the line to give the story a Triple-A production. (Mr. Zanuck paid me 42 bucks for acting in it, which may mean something but I don't know what.)

"Location" proved to be in the Chatsworth Mountains that stretch out North by Northwest not more than a good hop, skip, and a jump from Hollywood.

And what a location it was! The complete city of Ranchipur, India, as envisioned by Bromfield in his book, had been built here at a cost of more than $200,000. The sets spread over 18 acres. The palace (where I got myself the bad case of shakes) covered a city block and cost, so a technical man said, close to $75,000. Back of the city a dam had been built and back of the dam was five million gallons of water, which is a damsite more water than you may imagine until you find it coming at you at flood-time speed.

■ Well, we go to work Monday morning with Clarence Brown directing. And when I say "we" I mean about 3,000 extras, a herd of forty elephants, and the entire cast of principals. Dressed up to represent a native of India, about all I do that first day is to keep lifting 'em up and setting 'em down in the mud as I walk through the streets of Ranchipur, while I get drenched to the skin trying to duck one cloudburst after another. The rains had already came—and how! Two nurses, a studio physician, and several masseurs and masseuses kept constant vigil over all the principals and saw that they had rub-downs in portable dressing rooms after each shower.

The temperature of each star was carefully checked to guard against colds that might result in costly delays. I heard Director Brown say it was costing the studio better than $25,000 a day to shoot these location scenes. But as for me, the other 2,999 extras, and the elephant herd —well, we just let it rain. Come quitting time I was so full of raindrops inside and out that I asked Dr. C. A. Seyfarth, the studio physician, if he couldn't graft a pair of gills on me and maybe a few scales, but he was too busy worrying about the health of Mr. Power, Mr. Brent, Miss Loy and the rest of his high-salaried charges to worry about Mr. E. J. (The Old Umbrella Man) Smithson.

■ The second day was about the same as the first only the rains came harder and faster and colder, but I got along a little better because George Brent gave me one of his rubber shirts to wear.

And talking about George, I surely pitied that guy. The strong, silent Irishman who for eight years has lived through

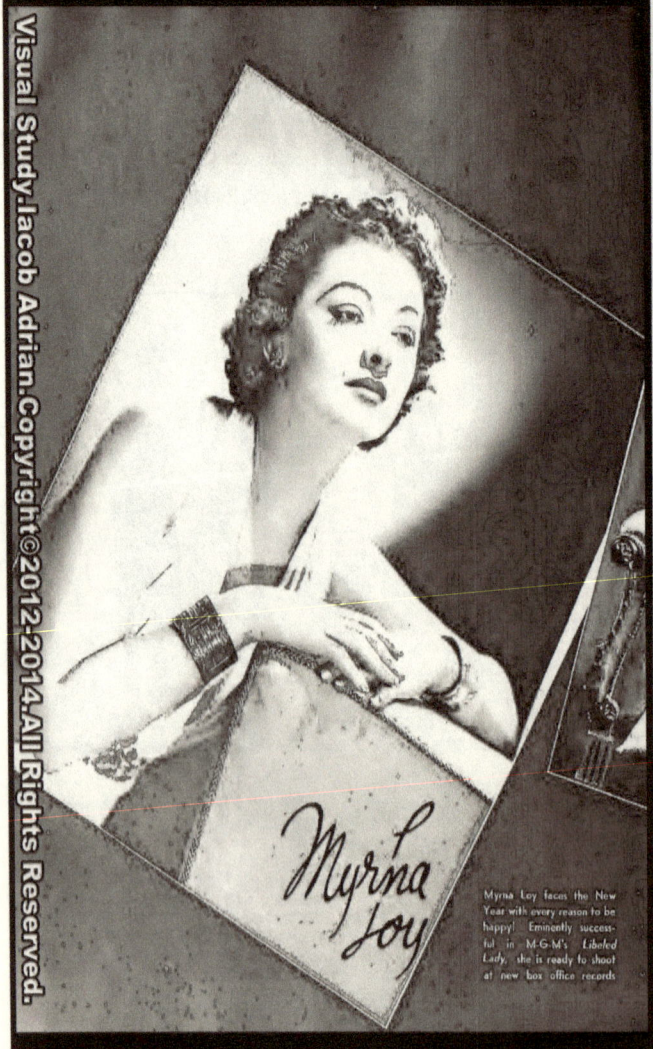

Myrna Loy faces the New Year with every reason to be happy! Eminently successful in M-G-M's *Libeled Lady*, she is ready to shoot at new box office records

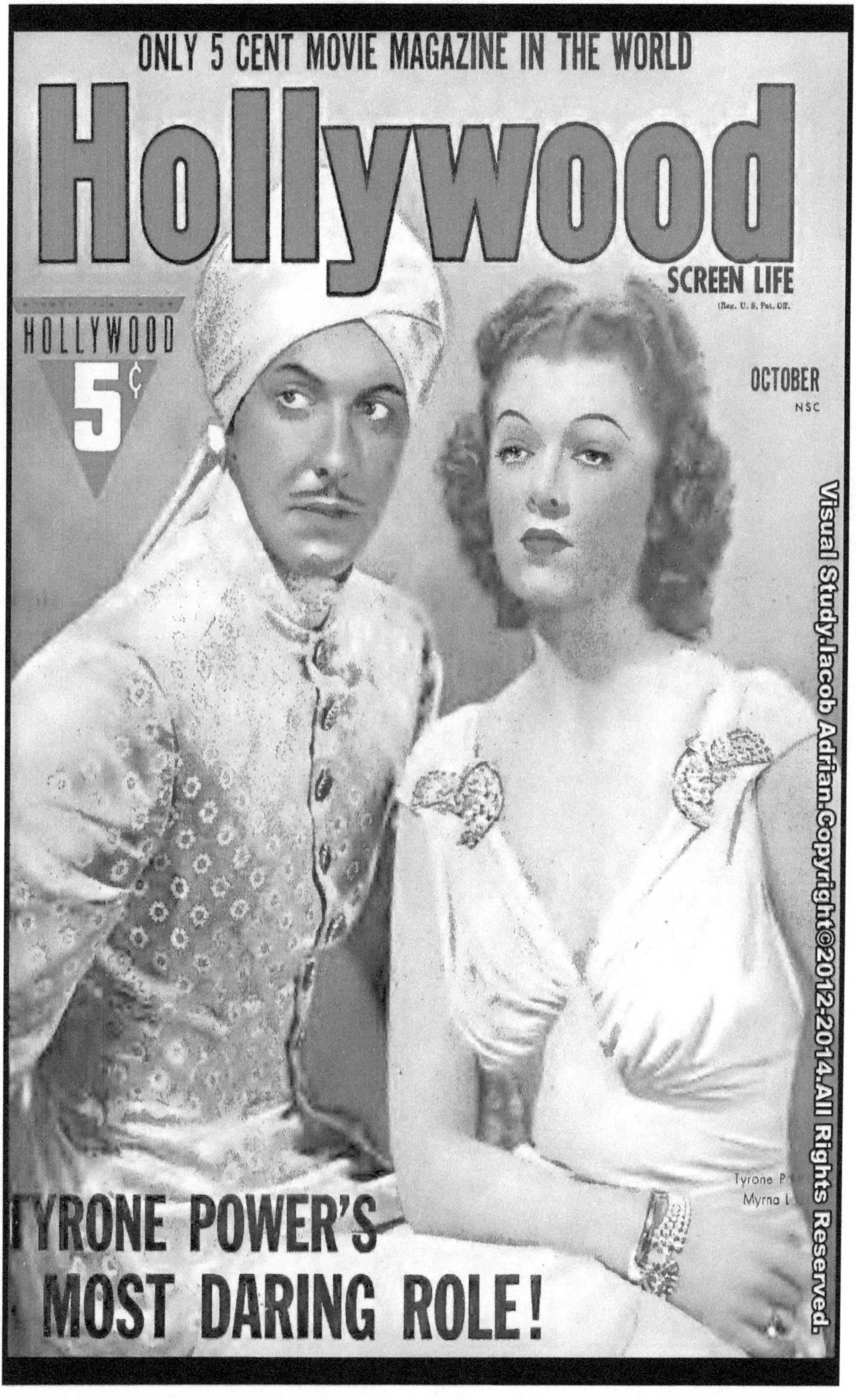

Hollywood

SCREEN LIFE

(Reg. U. S. Pat. Off.)

HOLLYWOOD

5¢

OCTOBER

NSC

Tyrone P
Myrna L

TYRONE POWER'S
MOST DARING ROLE!

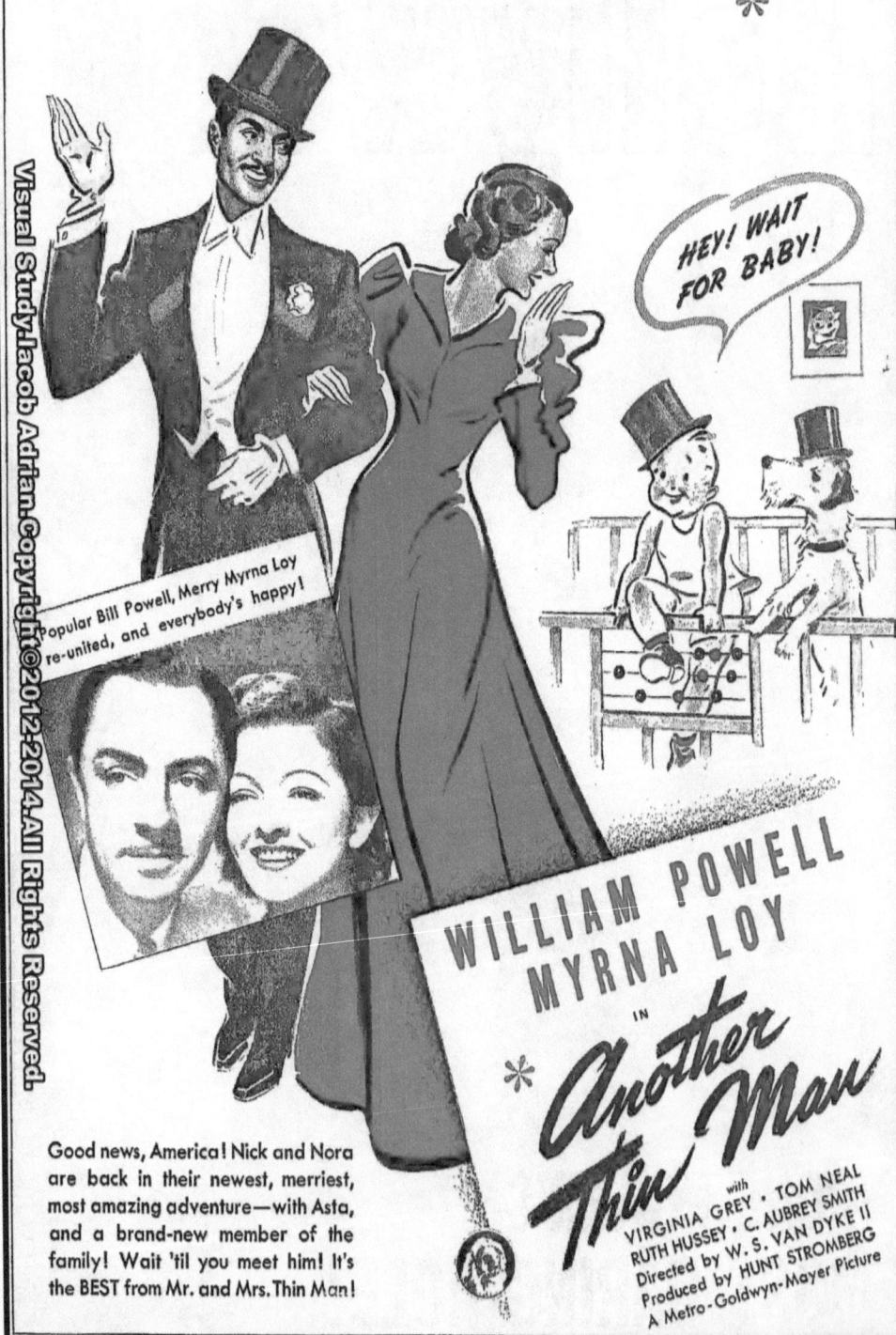

Baby Takes a Bow

By

EMILY NORRIS

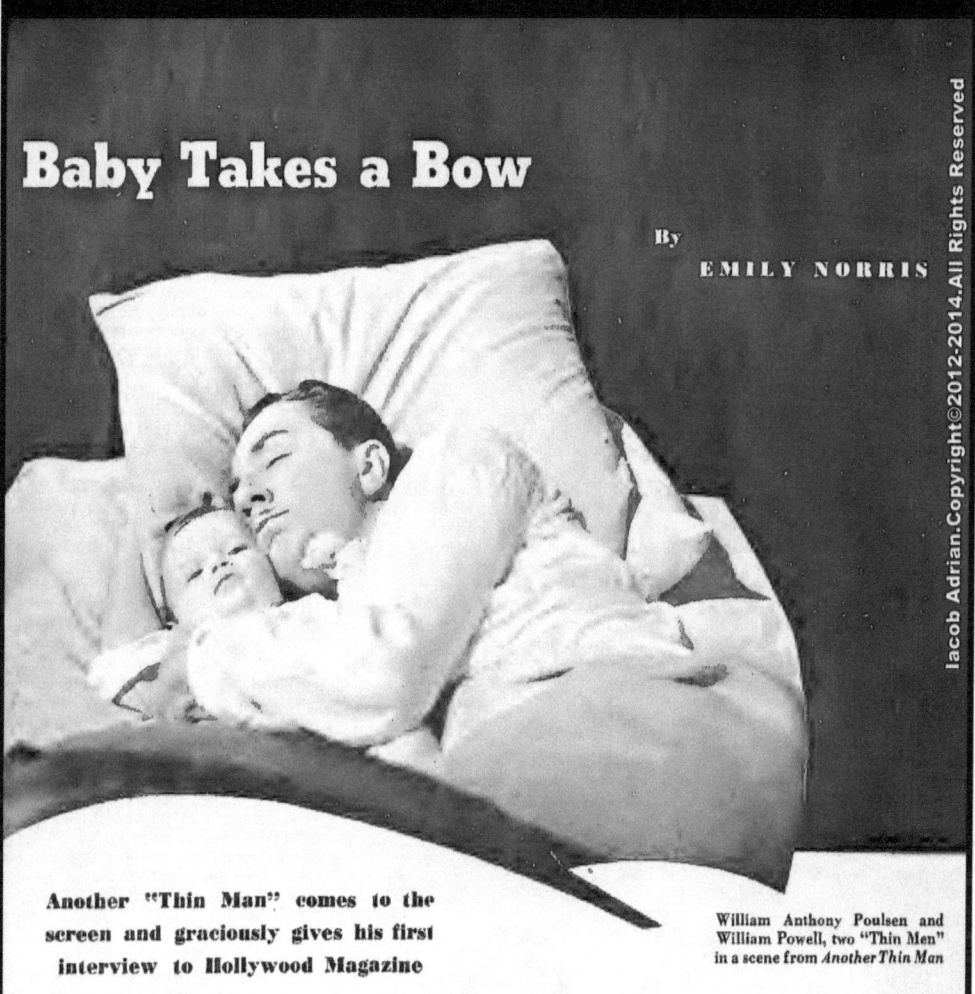

Another "Thin Man" comes to the screen and graciously gives his first interview to Hollywood Magazine

William Anthony Poulsen and William Powell, two "Thin Men" in a scene from *Another Thin Man*

It seems the underworld was giving the Thin Man's baby a party . . . . . . And park your guns outside, gents.

You remember how, in *After the Thin Man*, Myrna Loy sat knitting little pink things and Thin Man Bill Powell asked, "What're you knitting *those* for?" So Mrs. Myrna Thin Man said: "And you call yourself a detective!" Well, the eventuality in this new picture, *Another Thin Man*, is eight months' old "Cuddles." That is what the rest of the cast called him.

("A fine monicker for a detective's son!" Cuddles fumed in sign language when we had a moment alone. That is, alone with only a nurse or so and a representative of the Board of Education hovering around.)

Already the guests were arriving, and that corner of the M-G-M lot looked like a maternity ward. With sixteen babies scheduled for the party, of course they had to have forty-eight babies on hand. Huh? No, there's no mistake in mathematics. Count 'em yourself.

You see, the law allows a baby only so much time before the cameras and under the lights per day. Therefore, to expedite matters, sixteen of the first group of thirty-two infants acted as stand-ins for the other sixteen. The third group of sixteen were needed, because, according to law, the first group had to quit work by two in the afternoon.

To go with the forty-eight babies, there were forty-eight mothers, forty-eight nursing bottles, forty-eight "formulas," forty-eight sets of didies, eight studio nurses and a dozen gallons of milk. Before Director W. S. Van Dyke finished shooting the sequence he said he felt like a mother himself.

The idea was that the Thin Man, being a famous private detective, naturally had a lot of acquaintances who were pickpockets, gangsters, and what not, but who helped him out sometimes on his more difficult cases. In return for his kindness on many occasions when the world seemed against them, these acquaintances—hearing that the Thin Man had become a father—decided to throw a party (in a nice way) for his son and heir.

Each underworld character had been told to bring his own baby. And each did with one exception. He being babyless but eager to join in the festivities, rented an infant and passed it off as his own.

("This ought to be a warning to people not to go around renting babies," Cuddles confided, again in the sign language, as —rosy and smiling—he contentedly blew bubbles in his special dressing room while waiting to go on the set to act as host at the party. He raised tenuous eyebrows, mere fuzz really, at a particularly handsome bubble and added: "The consequences of that fellow's ill-considered baby-hiring—glub. Glub, glub, glub— you'll see, in due time.")

Now, the mugs (and that's the right word) who were giving the party had been picked by the casting director for their rugged features. Rugged? They looked as if they'd come through a blizzard of broken crockery. One by one the babes were handed carefully to these gentlemen an instant before the cameras turned.

The result, though unanticipated, was a

tribute to the infants' sense of civic righteousness even at their tender age. Without exception they took a look at the men designated in the script as their fathers—and burst into frightful howls of disapproval.

For probably the first time since talking pictures came in, nobody had to yell, "Quiet!" as the cameras rolled. The command wouldn't have been heard, anyway. Grips, juicers, extras, could not merely have conversed but given college cheers and still not been heard above that infant uproar. The mugs, pale beneath their makeup, looked terrified.

Things, though, had quieted down a trifle in the Thin Man's maple and cretonne living room, and Asta, the wire-haired terrier, was making friends with the guests while Myrna served cake and the Thin Man bragged about Cuddles, when word came that a cop was at the door. Well, you know how it is between cops and the underworld. The guests began to depart at once. In the excitement, the guest who had hired a baby picked up Cuddles, the Thin Man's child, in mistake for the baby he had hired.

("He left the rented baby, but Myrna and Bill didn't want it," Cuddles explained, placing his toe in his mouth. He went on smugly: "They liked me better." He omitted mention of the fact that the mother of the rented baby brought back Cuddles, fire in her eye, and demanded her own offspring in exchange. A nurse took Cuddle's toe from his mouth and put a nursing-bottle there instead. "Glub, glub," Cuddles murmured contentedly,

his bright eyes twinkling his thanks.)

There was always a nurse near Cuddles, of course. The baby got more care than Bill Powell himself. Part of the attention showered upon the baby was prescribed by statute. He could "work" only four hours a day. During the four hours he could spend only four minutes right under the lights. And he could spend these four minutes at the rate of only thirty seconds at a time.

Talk about a star! The baby ordered Myrna and Powell around with the greatest complacency. For instance, they had to be right there, all set for the scene, before the baby was brought on. No waiting! No wasting one of those thirty seconds! Fortunately, Director Van Dyke is a fast shooter.

Then there was the matter of castor oil. Oh, not taken internally. No. But drops of castor oil were put in Cuddle's eyes before a scene to form a film as protection from the lights. They were put in after a scene also, for good measure or something. And the instant the scene began, the city welfare worker from the Board of Education would stand with gaze glued on a watch. Just try to work the baby five seconds overtime!

The nurse, as well as mother, saw to it that Cuddles had his naps promptly, and his feedings—there was a little electric plate in the dressing room for heating milk. The dressing room was as scrubbed and sanitary as a hospital corner. No, the salary check didn't have to be sterilized.

("Myrna and Bill said," Cuddles remarked, "that it was quite an education

for them, watching me taken care of, and taking care of me. In the picture, they had to change my—ah—underthings. They didn't know how, at first." He gave a toothless grin. "I had to laugh.")

■ The entire cast laughed at Myrna and Bill somewhat later, though the laugh had nothing to do with Cuddles. It had to do with two surprise parties on the set, in addition to the one given to Cuddles in the script. Myrna and Powell have birthdays within a few days of each other, and three or four times it has happened that they worked in a picture together on those days. It's become increasingly hard for them to surprise each other, but this time they outdid themselves.

On his birthday Bill was about to go before the cameras when somebody told him that a Mr. Gwynn, friend of one of the M-G-M producers, was waiting in Bill's dressing room. "But I can't see him now!" Bill protested. "You must," the messenger insisted, "He's a friend of So-and-So." "All right," Bill said, exasperated, and rushed to his dressing room.

When he threw open the door, there stood a live penguin, dressed to resemble Powell, studying itself seriously in the mirror. Upon its back, turned toward the door, was a sign: "Happy birthday from one Thin Man to Another." Powell burst out laughing. "Well, he has my nose and chin," he remarked. On his return to the set, he found tables decorated and ready for the big party that followed the day's shooting.

Came Myrna's birthday, and she was determined to be surprised at nothing. But right away Bill surprised her. Nailed on her dressing room door that morning when she arrived was a great printed notice: "SURPRISE PARTY FOR MYRNA LOY—COME ONE, COME ALL!" At noontime, a town crier walked across the set, ringing his bell and announcing that there would be a surprise party for Myrna. In the course of the afternoon, they turned on the radio during a rest period and heard several local stations sing: "Happy birthday, dear Myrna" and announce a surprise party for her. By the time the party started, after the day's work, nobody in town including Myrna was unaware of the fact that Myrna was going to be very much surprised. Asta the terrier was at the party. So was Duke.

Duke is a huge Irish wolfhound when he stands on his hind legs, he is around seven feet tall. In one scene, he was supposed to greet Powell menacingly with his paws on Powell's shoulders. Powell loves dogs and vice versa. Duke, affectionate in proportion to his size, wouldn't menace. He insisted on trying to lick Bill's face. "In place of a necktie, I'll have to wear a strip of bacon so it'll look as if he were going for me," Powell suggested. [Continued on page 65]

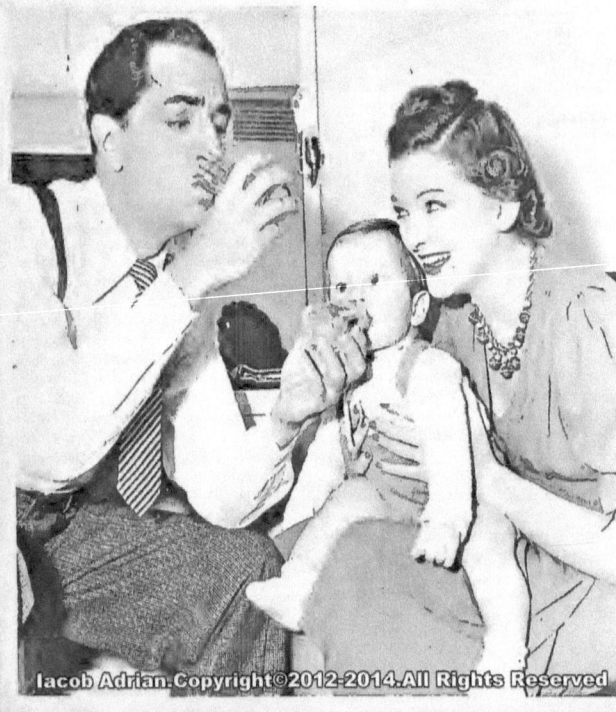

Myrna Loy manages the two "Thin Men" with admirable fairness in a scene from the newest comedy in the series

the new government. Fortunately, their Hungarian estates were left intact.

As he grew to young manhood, Ershi became increasingly bored with the idle, useless life of a young nobleman. At last he rebelled outright and announced he was leaving home to pursue his real ambition—the study of poster art—and to earn a name for himself.

Instantly the family purse strings were drawn tight. He was cut off without a penny so long as he chose to remain away from home.

After studying with Cassandre in Paris, where he lived frugally, and supported himself as best he could, he went to Stockholm for further study. There he won the first prize for poster art for two successive years at the art academy. By dint of saving and sacrifice, he acquired sufficient means to come to America with a modest bankroll. A New York stock promoter promptly sold the gullible young man a gold mine—*sans* gold—in New Mexico. Once more he was broke. It was then he met Pat.

For two years they romanced in a lighthearted, happy way. Her career was going through its humble beginning of bits and small roles in New York stage productions and his talent for unusual posters was gradually winning him a name in the commercial art field.

He asked her to marry him. With the proposal came an unexpected provision: if she became Countess Takatsny, she must give up all thought of being an actress. Acting wasn't done by Hungarian countesses in good standing.

Pat countered with a provision of her own: she would marry him in one year but meantime she wanted the chance to prove to herself one of two things. Either she had dramatic ability and could succeed, or she had no talent and no place in the theater. If she gave up without *knowing*, she felt she might harbor a nagging doubt and regret for what might have been.

Ershi understood and agreed. They became engaged on that basis.

Suddenly the picture changed. He received word of the death of his mother. Since his brothers were serving in the army, he must return immediately to settle the estate and take his place as head of the family.

"Break our pact," he urged Pat. "Marry me now and come home."

Pat was sorely tempted. She was discouraged at the little progress she seemed to be making and it was an alluring prospect offered her—wealth, position, a title, and a life of ease and fun. Still, some inner force would not let her compromise. Ershi sailed alone.

In three months he wrote, *demanding* an immediate decision on her part. With characteristic spirit she answered the demand. No. The Irish can be coaxed but not bullied.

The following Christmas a small package was delivered at her door. It carried no card. Inside was a slender steel ring with her initials in block, a design Ershi once had sketched in an idle moment. Inside were engraved the words:

"Good luck and happiness."

It was her last word from him. ∎

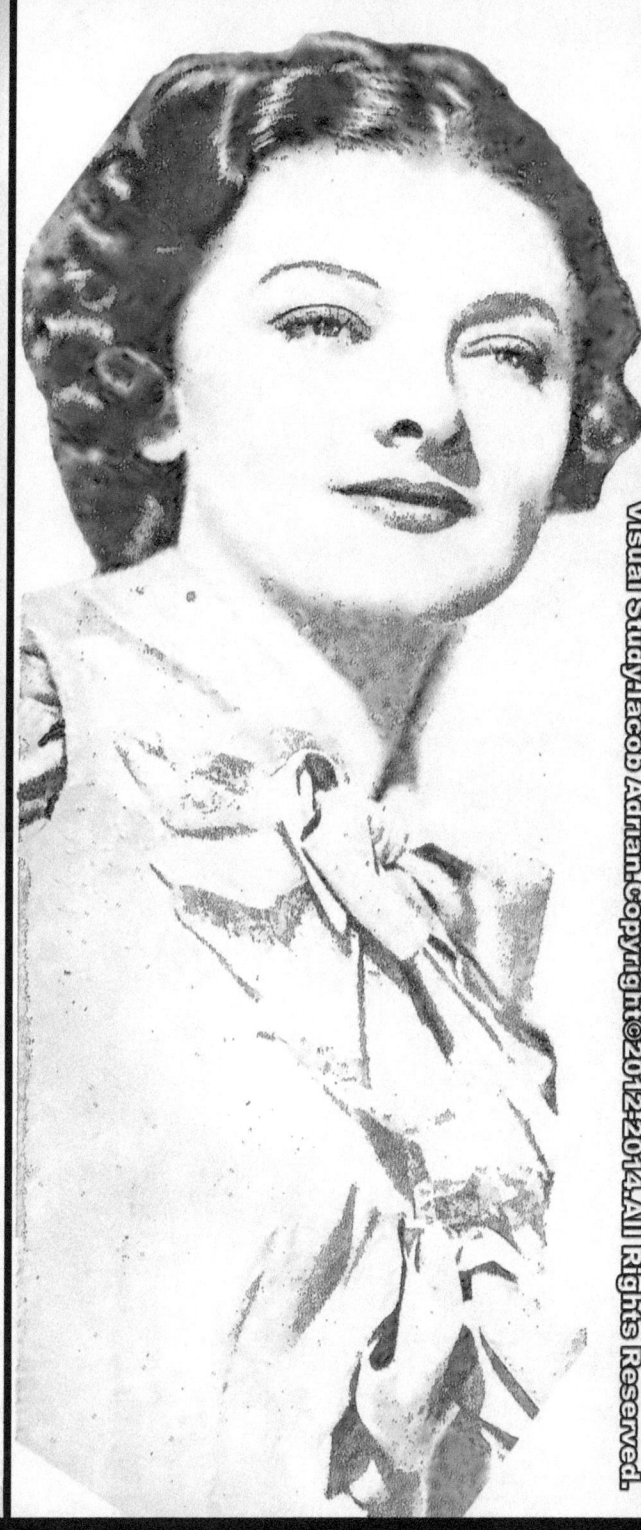

Bibliographic sources :

Hollywood (1934-1943)
Publisher: Hollywood Magazine, inc. ; Fawcett Publications, inc.

The New Movie Magazine (1929-1935)
Publisher: Tower Magazines, inc.

This documentary study use,
combined in various proportions,
elements from the following categories,
forms and subsets :
- fair use
- documentary
- documentary photography
- feature
- journalism
- arts journalism
- visual journalism
- photojournalism
- celebrity photography
in order to :
- employ material as the object of cultural critique ,
- quote to illustrate an argument or point ,
- use material in historical sequence,
providing independent opinion,
using photos, press articles, advertisements,
opinions of fans etc. ...